The True Tale of Charlie Plant

Written and Illustrated

by

Jane Sherwood

ISBN-13: 978-1-980-25126-2

All rights reserved. Copyright © Jane Sherwood 2018.

No part of this publication may be reproduced for commercial gain without the written permission of the author.

All the illustrations are montages created from the author's own drawings and photographs combined with public domain source material including drawings and paintings contemporary to the time. As far as the author is aware there are no copyright issues with the original source material and all rights are reserved on the final work.

Dedicated to Willow, Freya and River.

This biography is based on historical documents researched over the last twenty years along with anecdotal evidence gathered from family members. Some characters have been invented and others expanded to add weight to the story with a couple of name changes. My references to the history of Kingston-upon-Thames are gleaned from the archive at Kingston Museum and particularly the writing of June Sampson, both as a journalist for "The Surrey Comet" and from her book "The Story of Kingston" published in 1972. I have June to thank for the discovery that my ancestor, Samuel Gray, was a prominent Kingstonian with a road named after him. I also found "The Dictionary of the Thames" originally published in 1893 by Charles Dickens (son of the great Charles Dickens) an invaluable reference book for technical details and historical miscellany. The text is not intended to be an academic exercise, it is the story of a simple man and how he led his life. Any errors are of my own making.

Family Pedigree and Timeline.

JOHN COLLS (Charlie's great grandfather). 1744-1806
Quaker, yeoman farmer, corn merchant & miller in Norfolk.
ELIZABETH EVERARD (Charlie's great grandmother). 1746-1811
Married in 1768 & had 11 children between 1769-1788 including:

RICHARD H. COLLS (Charlie's grandfather). 1775-1836
London corn merchant and Norfolk mill owner.
SARAH HOOD ANSELL (Charlie's grandmother). 1780-1865
Married in 1802 & had 6 children between 1802-1818:
Richard (widowed art dealer, 2 children), Elizabeth & Joanna (spinsters), Ebenezer (married, marine artist, 7 children), **MERCY** (Charlie's mother), Lebbeus (married, artist & dealer, 7 children, including Walter L. Colls).

MERCY COLLS (Charlie's mother). 1815-1860
MICHAEL F. PLANT (Charlie's father). 1804-1863
Draper & silk mercer from Checkley in Staffordshire.
Married in 1836 & had 8 children between 1837-1855:
Mercy (spinster, housekeeper), Fred (widowed twice, clerk, 6 children), Joanna (married widower Mr Chamberlain, 8 children), James (married twice, mariner & upholsterer, 3 children), Sarah (spinster, laundress), Julia (spinster, laundress, barmaid), Ellen (died) & **CHARLIE**.

CHARLES C. PLANT Basketmaker and wherryman. 1855-1930
ALICE M. GRAY (Charlie's wife). 1856-1904
Married in 1877 & had 6 children between 1877-1893:
Mabel (died 1 yr), Florrie (died 3 yrs), **ANNIE,** Percy (married, dairyman, 3 daughters), Connie (married, servant) & Sid (married, cowman, 1son).

ANNIE M. PLANT (Charlie's daughter). 1885-1958
FRANK SHERWOOD (Charlie's son-in-law). 1889-1956
Married in 1913 & had 2 sons between 1913-1920:
Charlie (married, bookmaker, 1 daughter) & **PERCY.**

PERCY R. SHERWOOD (Charlie's grandson). 1920-1993
Precision Engineer & Chauffeur Car Hire Proprietor.
JOYCE CHESHIRE (Charlie's granddaughter-in-law). 1924-2000
Married in 1944 & had 1 daughter **JANE** in 1954.

Contents

I	The Birth of Charles Christopher Plant.	13
II	A Short History of The Family Colls.	15
III	Michael Plant Finds a Job & a Wife.	19
IV	Moving House & Raising a Family.	23
V	Bailiff to The High Court, Mr Samuel Southey.	27
VI	Moving to Kingston, a Wedding & Sad News.	31
VII	Charlie Settles At School.	37
VIII	W. Smith & Sons, Linen Drapers.	43
IX	Trouble at W. Smith & Sons.	51
X	A Fresh Start With New Friends.	57
XI	The Business of Basket Making.	63
XII	Derby Day & Several Proposals.	67
XIII	The Wedding & Other Celebrations.	73
XIV	Married Life & Fatherhood.	81
XV	Time to Move & Be Independent.	87
XVI	Annie May is Born Amongst Terrible Tragedy.	91
XVII	Oaklea Passage & Big Changes.	97
XVIII	Messrs Budden & Hart, Boat Builders & Watermen.	103
XIX	The Tolworth Tram & Lenelby Road.	109
XX	The Great War.	115
XXI	Charlie Plant's Greatest Achievement.	123

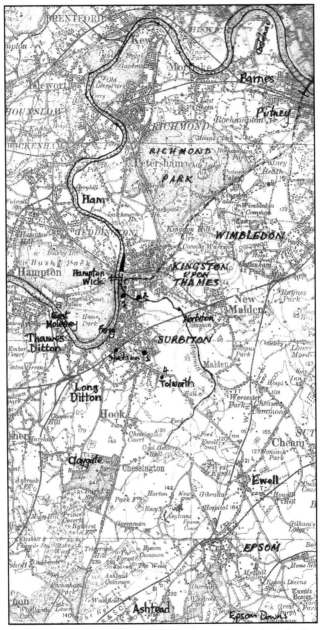

1. Browns Road. 2. Grange Passage. 3. Oaklea Passage. 4. Lenelby Road.

List of Illustrations.

	Map of Kingston-upon-Thames.	10
I	Romford Workhouse Infirmary.	12
II	Horstead Mill, Norfolk.	14
III	Mercy & Michael's Wedding.	18
IV	Calthorpe Place.	22
V	Bailiff Southey's House.	28
VI	Arrival at Clattern House.	32
VII	Charlie & Abe in the Schoolroom.	38
VIII	Christmas at the Linen Drapers.	44
IX	W. Smith & Sons Shop Window.	52
X	Sam Gray on a Thames Barge.	60
XI	Charlie at Work.	62
XII	Derby Day.	69
XIII	Bonfire Night in the Market Square.	72
	Signing of the Wedding Register.	79
XIV	Doctor Corbett with Alice & Mabel.	83
XV	Annies Cottages, Grange Passage.	86
XVI	Chas, Alice & Florrie at Richmond Park.	92
XVII	Jubilee Day at Canbury Gardens.	99
XVIII	Chas & Mr Colls at The Thames Hotel.	106
	Mr Colls Visiting Card.	107
XIX	Tram Terminus at The Red Lion.	108
	Lenelby Road, Tolworth.	110
XX	Auntie Connie, Baby Charlie and Annie.	117
	Letter from King George V.	120
XXI	Frank & the Pigeon Loft about 1928.	126
	Annie with Percy about 1930.	131

Chapter I

The Birth of Charles Christopher Plant.

It was a delightfully warm spring day on the fourth of May in 1855 but no sunshine could penetrate the dark and dreary infirmary at the Romford Union Workhouse. The winter had been long and hard, the coldest on record, the River Thames had frozen over and the Plant family were living in a small damp parish cottage at Haynes Terrace in Hornchurch. Michael Frederick Plant had lost his job and his family were surviving on meagre funds with the help of the parish. His wife was expecting her eighth child and suffering from consumption.

Mercy Plant was getting frequent pains, she was in the final stages of labour. She knew what to do, she was well practised in the art of child birth but her strength was fading. The ward was clean but bare, the nurses in their starched aprons and white bonnets were not attentive. The family were taking charity and could not afford better care. Charlie was born quickly and remarkably healthy considering the torment his mother had experienced while she was carrying him. Her previous child Ellen was born in the workhouse infirmary at Hornchurch, a frail four year old being cared for by her eldest sister, who also looked after the other children while their father was detained at a debtors' clearing house.

Mercy and her son Charlie remained as inmates in the infirmary for many months. The conditions were harsh but he knew no better and he loved his mother, who cuddled him as much as possible when the staff were not looking. When she became too weak to care for him his eldest sister, also called Mercy, took Charlie home and looked after him as best she could. He had no memory of his mother, she died in the workhouse infirmary, alone, just before Charlie's fourth birthday. None of her family were present at her death, her husband had been sent back to Staffordshire to find work and her children had been separated and placed in various different establishments by the Parish Union.

Horstead Water Corn Mill on the River Bure, Norfolk about 1820.

Chapter II

A Short History of The Family Colls.

Michael Plant was an attentive father, he had grown up in a large family and valued the affection and company of his own children. His eldest daughter Mercy named after her mother was now nineteen and they would both sit with the children recalling happy times when they lived in fashionable Calthorpe Place and had a house servant. They delighted in telling the younger children the same stories they had heard from Mercy, about her childhood in a grand household by the name of Colls.

Mercy's father, Richard Horton Colls, leased a large house in Tavistock Square and owned a great deal of land and property in Norfolk. Mercy grew up in the country at Horstead Mill surrounded by many brothers, sisters and several servants. The mill was owned and worked by her father and his father before him. They were Quakers and came from a long line of yeoman farmers, millers and corn merchants who were highly respected in the City of Norwich. John Colls, Mercy's grandfather, was an overseer at Norwich Corn Market and a Trustee of the Town Lands where he distributed his rent receipts to the poor. He was acquainted with the Gurney family and all business was carried out within the Quaker community. However, his son Richard did not favour country life and eagerly took on the London Corn Market trade. Richard preferred the big city to parochial Norfolk but still continued to run the mill after his father's death.

Although Mercy had a very privileged childhood, it was austere. Her Quaker family were simple people and did not approve of art, fashion and worldly pleasures. She studied bible reading, drawing and needlework in the Norfolk countryside each summer and when not at her lessons played in the gardens and met friends with her family at the Norwich Meeting House each Sunday. When Mercy was a little older she was allowed to accompany her parents to London during the winter months. She was fascinated by this different life that her father had clearly enjoyed as a younger man. She was attracted to the hubbub of the city and as a young lady would promenade along Bond Street with her sister to her favoured linen draper, "Kent & Bull" at number 164, a few shops away from where her brother later opened an Art Studio. She purchased fashionable cloth and trimmings and was always given special attention by the dapper Mr Plant.

On 27th April 1836 Richard Horton Colls died at home in Tavistock Square and left his entire estate to Sarah Hood-Colls, his:

> "Dear and affectionate wife."

To be distributed as she saw fit assisted by their eldest son Richard, Mercy's eldest brother. Sarah was distraught and went back to Norfolk to grieve, leaving her children who were all now grown up to remain in London. She was an ambitious woman who had married well and always strived to keep up appearances. She was born to a tenant farmer in Parndon, Essex and her mother died when she was born. Her father remarried and Sarah was brought up by her stepmother in a staunch Quaker household.

Mercy and her sisters, Elizabeth and Joanna, were given a small retainer and continued to live in Tavistock Square where they had the luxury of many servants. Richard was already married and Mercy's younger brother Lebbeus was lodging with him. Ebenezer was also married and busy making his own way as an artist. Her sisters, still spinsters, were much older and not interested in what Mercy was doing. This gave Mercy the opportunity to become better acquainted with her handsome beau, Mr Michael Frederick Plant.

Away from the stern eye of their mother, Mercy's brothers were rapidly becoming leading lights in the art world. Richard was a dealer for several artists including Edmond Gill and Samuel Palmer, he had a reputation for being ruthless and was also running his own print and engraving studio with Lebbeus. Ebenezer was an accomplished marine artist; his work was popular and sold well. Their lives were intertwined with Victorian High Society. Their Quaker faith conflicted with their interests and was side lined; they were not shy in using their contacts for commercial gain. They were all too wrapped up in themselves to notice what Mercy was doing and within four months Mercy and Michael were married.

Eventually Mercy's mother, Sarah, came back to London where she remained until her death in 1865. She was preoccupied with her son Richard, now a widower, who was sued by William Henry Fox Talbot (the inventor of photography) for using his calotype process without permission. In 1852 Talbot gained an injunction against Richard to prevent him making or selling photographs on paper. Richard refused to pay the court costs and absconded to America where his mother joined him, briefly. The family shares in the Pennsylvanian railway were cashed in to cover Richard's living costs and after a short trip to Paris he returned to England under an assumed name where he retired to the comfort of his daughter's home in Kensington.

Meanwhile, Ebenezer and Lebbeus continued their art practise in London. Lebbeus's son, Walter Lebbeus Colls, became a celebrated and wealthy photographer who lived at Castlenau just across the river in Barnes. Their sisters, Elizabeth & Joanna, never married. Joanna became her mother's companion and lived in Westminster and Hammersmith, even after her mother's death. Elizabeth, the eldest daughter spent her life visiting friends and relations, living on her own means, she had no desire or need to marry. They all lived a comfortable life and Mercy was not given a second thought.

Mercy was young, innocent and rebellious. Her secret liaisons with Mr Plant, who at more than ten years her senior was exciting. Mercy was of age and did not need parental consent to marry. She had no experience of finance or worldly matters and had lived a very sheltered life. She benefited from an annual allowance and convinced her fiancée that if he could not afford to keep them both, she could. When her mother and brothers discovered the relationship, it was already too late and they were not well pleased.

St. George the Martyr Church, Queens Square, Bloomsbury.

Chapter III

Michael Plant Finds a Job & a Wife.

Michael Frederick Plant was born in Checkley, near Cheadle in Staffordshire within walking distance of Upper Tean where J & N Philips & Co set up a company in 1747 to manufacture narrow linen tape. They built cottages with looms installed for their workers and were good employers. Later when steam driven jacquard looms were invented, a mill was built in Tape Street to house the new machines and Michael's family moved to a new cottage. They all worked in the mill. The Plants lived next door to Mr Goodall the bookkeeper and caretaker of Tean Mill and Michael's mother realised that her son had a chance to escape the factory toil by training with Mr Goodall. Mrs Plant was widowed with many children and went hungry to pay for her son Michael's apprenticeship to Mr John Philips to learn clerksmanship with his bookkeeper at the age of twelve.

Michael was a quick learner and his masters were kind. He learned a great deal under the tuition of Mr Goodall and was occasionally sent to Oakhill, (Mr Philips mansion) on errands. He was a lively lad and always interested to hear about his masters' travels to Manchester and London. When Michael finished his term, he was given the chance to see the towns and cities he had heard so much about, employed as a travelling salesman for J & N Philips & Co. His first job was to accompany Mr Philips to London with a suitcase of haberdashery samples and a list of customers. One of those customers was Mr Bull, a partner in "Kent & Bull Linen Drapers and Warehousemen". Michael made several journeys back and forth by stagecoach. The first time he travelled it was by first class but when he was journeying alone he could only afford to travel on the top and in the winter, it was bitterly cold and wet. It took two days to travel to London with an overnight stop at a coaching inn where he had to pay for his own food and lodgings. This ate into the money he earned as a linen mercer and when Michael was offered an in-house job at Mr Bull's shop in Bond Street he jumped at the chance. This was his opportunity to make his own way in the world and Mr Philips wished him well.

Young Mr Plant was living in modest lodgings a few yards from the shop and he loved the vibrant atmosphere that surrounded him. His new employment paid well and he was able to utilise all the skills he had learned as an apprentice clerk in the linen mill. The autumn was a particularly busy time when wealthy residents who owned town and country estates arrived for the season. Ladies and gentlemen would frequent the shop and promenade up and down the busy streets during daylight hours. At dusk the respectable clientele departed to their grand homes in Mayfair and Bloomsbury, the streets then filled with pleasure seeking fops and wastrels. It was well known that no lady of good breeding should be seen after dark in Bond Street, or the Piccadilly area and as Michael hurried home after work he soaked up the atmosphere with great delight.

Mr Michael Plant had been working at the shop for several years and was now senior assistant and clerk. His lodgings were comfortable and he always looked dapper in the most fashionable clothes. He tried to save a little to send back to Checkley but there was always something to spend his money on. He enjoyed good food and wine in moderation but never gambled. His employers found him to be conscientious and reliable with a mischievous personality that captivated their customers, not least, Miss Mercy Colls. She frequented his shop regularly when her father was ill and Mr Plant always asked after his health. Miss Colls soaked up his advice on choice of haberdashery and linens particularly when he told her which colours suited her best and those that complimented her beautiful eyes. When Mercy's father died she attended the shop even more frequently to purchase mourning goods and Mr Plant arranged their delivery to her dressmaker in Great Portland Street.

Mercy was grieving for her father and Mr Plant looked a little like him. Her mother had gone to Norfolk and her brothers and sisters were not interested in their young sister who they always thought too flighty. Mr Plant was a mature man who offered Mercy sympathy and fatherly support. She did not think the age gap to be strange, her mother married young to an older man and she always thought young men of her own age rather silly. Their relationship blossomed across the shop counter and very occasionally Mr Plant was able to leave the shop in the charge of his junior assistant while he met Miss Colls for afternoon tea. Mercy and Michael were both romantics and when Mr Plant proposed marriage they both agreed it should be kept secret. They did not need to elope, Mercy was of age and the wedding was arranged quickly and quietly by licence with Curate Benjamin Burgess, without the permission or knowledge of her mother Sarah, who was still in Norfolk.

Very few people attended St. George the Martyr Church at Queens Square, in Bloomsbury on Tuesday 1st September 1836. Mercy had commissioned a new afternoon dress with the help of her beau and looked beautiful in the pale blue silk with a French lace trim that Michael had presented to her. He had purchased the lace from his colleagues at "Tinkler & Co." in Old Bond Street. Michael had kept in touch with his family. His uncle William, a retired farmer and his youngest sister Caroline, who was only sixteen were thrilled to attend and be witnesses at the short simple ceremony. Mercy had no friends or relations present but she was very happy. The celebrations progressed with a fine luncheon and adjourned afterwards to Michael's respectable lodgings where a genteel gathering sang songs around the piano. The ladies drank tea and the gentlemen imbibed copious amounts of port wine.

Mercy was 21, married and expecting a baby. She was very excited at the prospect and on 15th December 1837 their first child was baptised Mercy Sarah Plant at St. James Church, in Piccadilly. The Prince Regent had just died and Victoria was ruling the country at the young age of 19, there was an air of optimism throughout London and further afield. It was time to move to a larger house, to make space for their growing family away from the hustle and bustle of the fashionable but often rowdy West End.

7 Calthorpe Place, St. Pancras Borough.

Chapter IV

Moving House & Raising a Family.

The Plants both enjoyed living in the city and Mercy did not want to move far from where she grew up in Bloomsbury. They found a smart Georgian town house in the fashionable neighbourhood of Calthorpe Place only a short distance from Michael's workplace in Bond Street. The house had been built twenty years earlier and was a smart red brick terraced building with a railed basement, round headed doors and windows with three storeys above including an attic. Michael managed to secure a short lease at £40.00 per year. The family moved in and took on an experienced housekeeper called Eliza Waller who lodged in the attic. Mercy and Michael were very happy mingling with the smart London set. Mercy had made her own friends with whom she would meet for tea and then shop in the most fashionable establishments. Mr Dickens had just published a novel called "Oliver Twist" and Michael rushed out to purchase a copy before it sold out. Mercy would read it aloud to Michael in the evenings after supper and they both revelled in the excitement of the plot and pitied poor Oliver, an orphan who had fallen among thieves.

On Thursday, 28th June 1838 Victoria was crowned Queen of England. The crowds lined the streets and the Plant family were in that crowd at Piccadilly. A daily newspaper described the scene:

> "The procession passed along Piccadilly, whilst the liveliest demonstrations of affection fell upon Her Majesty's ears. The merry pealing of the bells and the shouts of the rejoicing people were exhilarating and truly delightful. From Piccadilly the procession passed into St. James's Street and Pall Mall, the balconies of the club-houses were thronged with elegantly dressed ladies, and others, cheering and waving their handkerchiefs."

Two years later Victoria married Albert on 4th February 1840, another exciting royal event that gripped London. Mercy and Michael watched the spectacle from Piccadilly and celebrated with a formal dinner for their friends at their Georgian town house. Their housekeeper Eliza arranged for 3 girls to come in and help with the preparations and service of the extravagant menu. Mercy and Michael were blissfully happy and Frederick Richard Plant was born exactly nine months later. Mercy was delighted to be with child the same time as the Queen, Princess Victoria was born the following month and Mercy could not have been more in vogue.

Just like the Royals, several children followed in the Plant household: Joanna Hannah, James Samuel, Sarah Bella and Julia Mary. The family was not large by Victorian standards but costly to keep when there was only one breadwinner. Mercy was rather careless with money and too well bred to work herself. The children needed educating, clothes were expensive and a servant was considered essential. Michael was still working as senior assistant and clerk at the linen drapers but his wages had not risen since his marriage. There was a lot of new competition from the large shops in Regent Street and the new factory production methods were making all textiles as well as other goods much cheaper, with less profit for the small draper.

The lease on 7 Calthorpe Place was due to run out for the third time and the bills were mounting. Their eldest daughter Mercy, was thirteen and expected to help out with the younger children, particularly new born baby Julia. The boys had a tutor for arithmetic, history and geography. Mrs Plant read a lot to all her children and taught them reading and writing. There was some tension in the household because their father was worrying about money. In order to reduce their costs Michael persuaded Mercy to find a house away from the city. They started out at 44 Camden High Street, then 15 Harrington Street and in January 1850 they moved into number 6 Hawley Terrace, a new house built in Georgian style by the Earl of Southampton in the centre of Camden village. This rural suburb was pleasant enough with a National School for the children, wide roads and green fields. Their neighbours were mainly retired people and tradesmen. The house had three storeys and they employed another Eliza, a young cheerful house servant to do all the cooking and cleaning.

Mercy was carrying her seventh child when disaster struck. Her husband came home from work unusually early one Wednesday in the summer of 1851 and announced that he no longer had a job. His employers had been struggling for a while and now had been declared bankrupt. There was no redundancy pay and his last month's wages were frozen. Michael wrote to his previous employer Mr Philips of Upper Tean in the hope he could gain employment with the company that trained him. Mr Philips responded by return, explaining that the company had been laying off staff at Tean Mill but he remembered the young Michael and his gift for selling and offered him a casual placement as a travelling salesman, a silk mercer, with payment by commission only. Michael was grateful but disappointed. This new occupation required him to trail the London streets visiting dressmakers, haberdashers and drapers plying his wares as a common hawker.

It was becoming apparent even to Mercy that the family could not continue spending money they did not have. Her allowance that she thought so generous when she married was not enough to cover even the basic necessities of life now they had a large family to support. In desperation, she wrote to her mother asking for help but events rapidly took over and the bailiffs arrived at their door for non-payment of rent. Initially they took items of furniture and clothing as payment but the family were warned they had one month to raise the funds owed or they would be evicted. The family were now living under the auspices of Romford Union in Haynes Terrace, Hornchurch. They had been moved out from Camden under the instruction of Mercy's cousin, a Quaker preacher who worked with the poor at St Olaves in Shoreditch. This was the most help that Mercy would get from her wealthy and influential family.

On 11th September 1851 Mercy gave birth prematurely to Ellen Emily Plant in a public ward at Hornchurch Union infirmary. Mercy was unwell and her daughter tiny and frail. The older women did their best to help in the labour room but they were untrained and inadequate. There were no nurses, the lying-in ward next door was crowded with mothers, babies and toddlers. The atmosphere was dark, damp and dirty with rags drying on the grate by the open fire. Kettles and pans hung above with gruel, laundry and boiling water all mixed up together. There were several cribs but only four beds, two wooden chairs and some benches. The screams of mothers in childbirth joined the crying of babies and toddlers to create an ungodly atmosphere of fear and misery.

Mother and baby were well enough to leave the infirmary after a few weeks and her eldest daughter, now fourteen, nursed her and took care of the other children while Mercy suckled baby Ellen. Michael had taken temporary lodgings in Oxford Street to carry out his work as a silk mercer during the week and each Sunday he tried to visit his wife and children. Hornchurch was eighteen miles east bound into Essex. He would start out early Sunday morning walking and taking his chance with the passing traffic. There was often a horse and cart going in his direction with a friendly drover who welcomed a bit of company. His return in the evenings were quite dangerous with highwaymen and vagabonds lying in wait on the dim dark roads to London. Michael preferred to wait until first light the following morning when he could catch the farm lads taking their produce and livestock to market along the Romford Road towards London at the beginning of the working week.

Despite all their hardship and Mercy's ill health she fell pregnant again in 1854. Her husband was still working away from home and visiting when he could. He was earning just enough to keep them all out of the workhouse and himself away from debtors' prison. Their eldest daughter, now considered an adult in the eyes of the Parish Union, was looking after all her brothers and sisters apart from Fred who had just been found an apprenticeship at Peter Robinson in Oxford Street. As their mother swelled with the baby she struggled to pick up even little Ellen who was now three but very small for her age. She relied heavily on her daughter Mercy who at the age of 16 was very competent and well able to look after Joanna, James, Sarah, Julia and Ellen in their tiny damp cottage.

In December, their father received a letter from Mr Philips saying his services were no longer required; the company was changing the way they sold their products and they had no need for travelling silk mercers. Mr Plant vacated his lodgings in Oxford Street and moved back in with his family with no income other than a small annuity that had been put in place for his children. The whole family managed to stay at Haynes Terrace while Mercy was pregnant by using their eldest daughter's money to pay the rent and buy food. When Michael took his wife to the infirmary to give birth to Charlie, their daughter Mercy was left in charge of the children and given responsibility for her own money. Her father was a debtor and any money that crossed his hands was immediately seized by the bailiff.

Charles Christopher Plant was born very quickly, he was his mother's eighth child and even though she was weak with consumption, he was a healthy baby boy. Mercy was never to come out of the infirmary, Charlie stayed with her for the first few years of his life and when she was too ill to look after him, his sister took him home with her. He had no memory of those times and only his mother would have known how hard their life was. Their father had left his children to avoid seizure of his eldest daughter's funds and taken lodgings at The Essex Buildings, where he shared a small dark dirty room with several other men. On Saturday, 7th February 1857 he was declared insolvent and made a resident at Western Road, Romford, a clearing house for debtors where Bailiff Samuel Southey was overseeing his case. His only consolation was that he had saved his children from the workhouse and his beautiful daughter Mercy was looking after them all, Joanna, James, Sarah, Julia, Ellen and Charlie while he was detained and their mother remained very ill in the Romford Union infirmary.

Chapter V

Bailiff to The High Court, Mr Samuel Southey.

In 1857 when Mercy was 20 she was caring for all her brothers and sisters apart from Fred and being overseen by the High Court Bailiff, Mr Samuel Southey. Their father Michael had been sent back to Staffordshire to look for work. His sister Caroline had found him a job with a distant relative working as a journeyman butcher's assistant. The small amount of money he was able to earn was sent back to Samuel Southey to help fund the placement of his children.

Mr Southey, High Bailiff to the County Court and Romford Union Gaoler was resident at North Street in the parish of Havering-atte-Bower in Essex. It was a large house with cells in the basement, next door to the vicarage. Both properties were owned by the Church and served the parish. Southey was a self-important man of tall stature born in 1780 to a landed Surrey family of Hampton Wick. He had great influence within the parish and regularly attended court proceedings as an official witness.

The future of the eldest son Fred was already accounted for. He was nearing the end of his apprenticeship and had acquired a range of useful skills to keep him employed. He lodged at Peter Robinson with many other employees including John Lewis who later went on to set up his own shop in Oxford Street. It was an exciting place for a young man and although he missed his family he enjoyed the life and had good pals in his workplace.

Joanna was two years younger and when her father's insolvency was announced, the parish considered her to be an adult and arranged a residential placement in Great Portland Street as an assistant dressmaker. This again was through her father's contacts in the trade. It came as a great shock to Joanna, because her eldest sister Mercy had never worked and she was a little resentful, but she made the best of it and was able to visit her brother Fred in Regent Street on her days off.

James was 11 years old in 1857 and the disruptive life of moving from place to place in increasingly difficult circumstances, affected him greatly. He was 14 when his mother died, his father had left for Staffordshire and the whole country was in mourning for Prince Albert, who had just died from typhoid. James barely knew his little brother Charlie and missed his big brother Fred. His mother had told him exciting stories about her uncle from Lowestoft who had sailed with Lord Nelson.

Romford Union Gaol & Sponge House, North Street, Havering-atte-Bower.

When Mr Southey suggested James could "go to sea", he jumped at the chance. He was immediately assigned to a cargo ship bound for New York as a novice apprentice seaman.

Sarah was only 12 when her mother died and distraught at being sent out to work away from her sisters as a servant for a veterinary surgeon in Saint Marylebone. Although the life was hard it was marginally better than being in the workhouse and the parish were keen to reduce their costs. Samuel Southey had a long list of potential employers wanting cheap labour, a servant girl of only twelve years would be the cheapest of them all. Sarah did not stay long with her employer, she missed her family so dreadfully that she ran away and followed them to Kingston, as we shall see later.

Finally, in the spring of 1861 it was time to place Charlie and his sisters. Julia now 11 and Charlie nearly 6 were at separate schools. Bailiff Southey had arranged for their sisters Mercy and Ellen to stay at his residence. This was a sponge house where visitors paid one pound per night for food and shelter as an alternative to being gaoled in his basement. The money paid went into the bailiff's personal coffer and was an extremely profitable sideline for the elderly gentleman. This arrangement was also his insurance for their father to keep in contact while Bailiff Southey organised the transfer of the children to Kingston-upon-Thames in Surrey.

Little Ellen now 9 and still very frail was a good companion for Mr Southey's daughter Julia aged 7. Her mother had recently died and Samuel at the age of 80 was on the lookout for his fourth wife. He was hopeful that Mercy aged 24 may be suitable. He also employed a young servant girl called Maria who carried out all the household duties. The bailiff always surrounded himself with pretty ladies and some years later married Rebecca, an attractive but rough illiterate female, 37 years his junior. He had an unhealthy liking for young ladies but Mercy was a strong character and resisted all his advances, she was keen to make her own way in the world.

Charlie had no memory of his time in the workhouse and only a few recollections from living with his sisters in Romford. He did however remember very clearly the day he and his sisters were taken to Kingston-upon-Thames. Where the sinister Samuel Southey was born and grew up within a very privileged family who were well respected within the borough.

Chapter VI

Moving to Kingston, a Wedding & Sad News.

Just after Charlie's sixth birthday on Tuesday the 7th May 1861 the Romford Board of Guardians called a meeting with Bailiff Southey and the churchwarden. The matter to discuss being the debtor Michael Plant and his dependent family. The bailiff reported on Mercy and Ellen and the churchwarden on Julia and Charlie. It was noted that Mr Plant had temporary employment in Staffordshire and his daughter Mercy had private funds that rendered her independent and therefore not liable to the parish. Mercy was unable to look after them all and reluctantly agreed that Julia, Ellen and Charlie should be transferred to Kingston where they could all board at the public schools if she paid a small fee in the absence of her father.

Early the following morning Mr Southey's assistant arrived at North Street in a hay cart. The children had been given a meagre breakfast and handed a bread roll each for their journey. Mercy was not there to say goodbye. Julia seemed older than her eleven years and immediately took charge of her nine year old sister Ellen and six year old Charlie. It was a cold morning with a gentle breeze but after a while the sunshine warmed the cheeks of the children as they watched eagerly to see where they were going. They were charity children not paupers, they had warm clothes and were carrying all their worldly possessions in a large Gladstone bag that had belonged to their mother. The adventure had begun. Their eldest sister had explained they were going to a boarding school where they would make new friends and learn lots of interesting things. Their father and brother Fred would visit them as soon as they could.

It took several hours to drive from Romford to Clattern House on the River Thames at Kingston. Old Bill the driver was rather gruff but he was kind to the children and his horse, called Billy. They trotted past Ilford, then Stratford but when they reached the Mile End Road it was busy with market traffic and their progress became slower and slower as they approached the city. They drove near Regent Street where brother Fred was working and along the north bank of the Thames at Westminster where their mother had lived before she married. After an hour or so they arrived at Putney Bridge but had to wait to cross through the heavy traffic. The children were agog, the scene was alive with activity. The river had barges, clippers, cargo ships and small fishing boats with wherrymen everywhere, rowing people and goods from one side to the other. The road was cluttered with open carts carrying hay, food and livestock to market. Hansom cabs with smart horses were driving gentlemen to their employment at the Houses of Parliament and into the city. Stage coaches were crammed with passengers and dozens of people of assorted class and denomination dodged in and out of the traffic with lots of shouting and shaking of fists.

Once they had crossed Putney Bridge they made faster progress as most of the traffic was coming towards them. The children had never been south of the river and Surrey appeared to be a prosperous place. There were a few grand houses on the way but mainly open fields and parkland, Putney Heath, Wimbledon Common and Richmond Park were all on route and soon after they had finished the last of their bread rolls they arrived in Kingston. Every day was market day here and the streets were crowded, just like London.

Bill and his horse knew the town well and wove in and out of the crowds, back down to the river bank and then a quick left turn brought them sharply to Clattern House, the municipal buildings and courthouse. Old Bill tethered Billy to a water trough stationed very conveniently by the entrance to the Law Courts and told the children to wait while he scurried off to find a porter. Within a few minutes he was back with the bell boy, a lad aged about fourteen and dressed in a grubby short black jacket, trousers and a pill box hat. The children disembarked, thanked Bill for a pleasant journey and followed the bell boy into the building where a large matronly woman wearing a starched white apron was waiting to greet them. She looked them all up and down, then shuffled them into a large room where three men were sitting behind a long high table. This was the Board of Guardians. The senior magistrate wearing a large white wig was seated in the middle and spoke first:

> *"I have been notified by Bailiff Southey that you are to be sent to the Public Schools in our parish. If you behave and learn your lessons you can do well, if you do not, you will be punished and returned to Romford Union Parish. Charles Christopher Plant, you will be sent to Richmond Road Boys School. Julia Mary Plant and Ellen Emily Plant you will be sent to Richmond Road Girls School. Do you have any questions?"*

The children remained silent and Mrs Ribbins was signalled to remove them from the chambers.

Charlie was lonely, he worked hard and learned his lessons well, longing for the day his father would visit. Fred was in touch with their father who could no longer work and was homeless. He had written to Fred to arrange lodgings for him in London and an affordable boarding house was found in Ernest Street, not far from Regent Street where Fred still lived and worked. These lodgings were poor indeed with dozens of men crowded into small rooms, not enough bedding and little furniture. Many of the men were ill including Michael who had paralysis from a stroke. He would sit at a large trestle table downstairs for most of the day unaware of his surroundings. It was only one step up from the workhouse and Fred was paying the rent.

Fred and his sister Mercy did their best to hold the family together, they were young and inexperienced with just a few memories of happy times to keep them going. The younger children knew their father was ill and he would not be visiting them. Fred also received one short letter from his brother James that had taken several months to arrive.

> *"Dear Fred.*
>
> *Arrived safely in New York where I jumped ship, I did not take to the navy and will not be going back. Tell father I have found a job in the silk trade and will not write again for fear of being caught. Just wanted to let you know I am alright.*
> *With kind wishes to all.*
>
> *James."*

During this time Fred had completed his apprenticeship and was now a qualified draper's clerk with a wage increase at Peter Robinson. Lodgings were still included, it was a very lively place and he had made many friends. The young ladies employed by the company lodged on the floor above and although the rules were draconian there was sometimes the opportunity for a social gathering at one of the numerous public houses in Regent or Oxford Street. Fred was rather taken with a Welsh lass called Betsy, a fancy goods assistant who worked front of house and they started walking out together. Betsy was a kind girl from a very close family and always provided a sympathetic ear for Fred's tales about his family troubles.

The Kingston Board had Frederick Plant (Charlie's eldest brother) listed as the family guardian. On 17th February 1863, something dreadful happened. Little Ellen, Charlie's youngest sister and only eleven years old, fainted and died. The town clerk Mr William Carter as the acting coroner held an inquest three days later and found cause of death to be "Natural sudden syncope". Ellen had been suffering from consumption and her small body had lost the strength to fight. The officials were very familiar with children dying in their care and their paperwork was often not up to scratch. Mr Carter had no personal knowledge of Ellen and on the advice of the senior coroner he entered her father's name as Frederick Plant instead of Michael F. Plant. The death was registered the following day and her small fragile body was bundled into a laundry basket and taken off for burial at Bonner Hill, with just a few prayers read by the chaplain in the presence of Julia, who was tearful and angry. Charlie was considered to be too young to attend and was not told of his sister's death until after the funeral. Ellen was laid to rest in pauper's grave number 31 and the cemetery records listed her name as Emily, nobody in authority cared. That evening during recreation, Julia wrote to her sister Sarah.

Fred was worried about Charlie and deeply upset by his sister's death. It fell upon him to tell his father, who did not take the news well. The shock triggered another stroke rendering him paralysed and unable to speak, he was deteriorating rapidly. Fred decided there was no time to waste, he asked Betsy to marry him, they arranged the wedding for Friday 27th March, the week before Easter at All Souls Church in North Regent Street. Betsy's father and sisters travelled up from Wales. Fred's sister Joanna who was still working around the corner in Great Portland Street, was able to attend and so were Mercy, Sarah, Julia and Charlie. Many of their friends and colleagues from Peter Robinson were also there and a grand day was had by all, a proper family gathering.

The Court of Assembly were advised by the chief clerk, Mr James Harmsworth about Ellen's death and they all agreed that it would be a good thing for Julia and Charlie to go to their brother's wedding. Sarah had left her job with the veterinary surgeon and travelled with Mercy to Kingston where they took lodgings at The Two Brewers in Wood Street, a cheap establishment run by Miss Neale, a respectable innkeeper. Bright and early on the day of the wedding Mercy met Charlie and Sarah met Julia at their respective schools in Richmond Road and walked to Kingston railway station at Town End in time for the eight-o-clock train to Waterloo Bridge.

Charlie was very excited, he had heard about steam trains and seen pictures and now he was going to travel on one.

Mercy purchased four third class return tickets to London at 1/8d each, a total of 6/6d, more than one week's wages for Mercy. They waited patiently at the very end of the platform. The train was about twenty minutes late but the hooting of the horn heralded its presence long before its arrival. The huge engine loomed out of a cloud of steam and smut with a great deal of shouting and activity. Charlie was dumb struck. There was only one third class carriage at the very back. Just the four of them boarded the narrow wooden truck, there were no windows or roof and they settled themselves on the wooden bench. The train started rolling after a whistle and several hoots, off they went faster than Charlie had ever been in his life. The carriage rocked violently from side to side and juddered up and down over the rails. The countryside flew past at great speed and each time they stopped Charlie was thrown forward across to the other side and back, bumping his head each time. When the train accelerated a shower of molten ash fell into the carriage which they quickly brushed off their clothes. It only took a few minutes to get to Wimbledon where more passengers boarded and goods trucks were loaded to the brim with vegetables, straw, several sheep and a couple of hogs for the London markets. This took nearly an hour and then they were off again at high speed and after stopping twice more they arrived at Waterloo.

The youngsters alighted from the train with Mercy leading the way, Sarah took charge of Charlie and Julia followed along beside. It was two miles to the Church, they sauntered over Waterloo Bridge frequently stopping to look at the boats, skipped through Piccadilly and ran up Regent Street along the same route that their parents had trod many years earlier. The wedding was enjoyed by all and the family were happy to be together but for Charlie, the train was the best experience and far outweighed the wedding celebrations. They returned home on the last train, the carriage was crowded like sardines with no room to fall over or sit down but their fellow passengers were a cheery bunch and they arrived back in Kingston soon after nine-o-clock at the end of a happy and momentous day.

Two weeks after Fred and Betsy married, Michael Plant died. Fred was present and sent a telegram to Mercy and to Joanna. They gave their father a respectable funeral but could not afford the burial so he went to an unmarked grave just like his wife and daughter before him. Mercy and Sarah were still lodging in Kingston and told the younger children. Charlie was sad again but he was getting used to his family disappearing, he never really knew his father and life carried on much the same. They were now all orphans and the younger children in the total charge of the Board of Guardians, or were they? The confusion over Fred being Ellen's father was an intentional error by Mr Harmsworth, who had been made aware by Bailiff Southey that the family had private funding. If Ellen had been listed as an orphan the other children would have been also, but for a substantial fee he could help them all. Mr Harmsworth was genuinely concerned for the family and did what he could to help, but he was not willing to work for nothing.

Mercy had secured a position as housekeeper to a widowed tradesman with three young children back in Westminster and wanted to ensure her sisters were looked after. Mercy and Fred visited Mr Harmsworth at his office in West-of-Thames Street, an ancient timber building that hung perilously over the river with water lapping the foundations. The Plant family money was signed over and put into the Post Office Savings Bank to be overseen by Harmsworth Solicitors. A document was drawn up making Sarah responsible for her brother and sister when she reached full age at 21. Until that date Mr Harmsworth had guardianship and control of the funds. Sarah was found an inside job as a laundress at Julia's school in Richmond Road. Julia was secured an apprenticeship in "women's work" to be taken up the following year when she was of age at 14, even though she was already working in the laundry as part of her education. Arrangements were made for Charlie to train as an apprentice draper somewhere in Kingston town when he was also of age. With their work done, Fred and Mercy said their goodbyes to the children and returned to London.

Chapter VII

Charlie Settles At School.

It was a very hard life for Charlie at school but he was luckier than many and he knew no different. He was popular with the other boys and he made friends easily which was just as well because frequently a friend would disappear without trace or become ill and go into the infirmary never to return, with no explanation. He saw his sisters once a week when all the scholars and staff assembled at Kingston Hall for Sunday prayers and teaching, but Charlie rarely got a chance to speak to them.

Charlie was only six when he was sent to the Boys Public School on the Richmond Road. He shared a bed with three other boys in a long, crowded dormitory. The nights were disturbed with constant coughing, sighing and crying from boys having bad dreams but Charlie was always exhausted and usually slept through. The master would check every evening at nine o clock to make sure all was quiet. If there was a boy whimpering in his sleep he was removed from the dormitory, disciplined and then returned with the threat of the birch. Most of the boys helped each other out and pretended to be asleep to avoid the master's wrath but there were a couple of trouble makers who bullied some of the younger boys and told tales. Charlie kept his head down, he was small in stature but a strong little character and had learned at a very young age how to stay out of trouble.

Abe who was two years older than Charlie had also come from the workhouse in Romford. He was tall for his age with a friendly face and snub nose, he had strong arms and long lanky legs that bowed at his knees. Abe stuck up for the younger boys and Charlie was often at his side, half his height and very skinny. When the masters were not around Abe would sing a song while Charlie danced a jig, a comical sight that made the other boys laugh. Abe talked of adventures on the seven seas that his seafaring father had told him. The younger boys were so eager to hear more stories that sometimes he would make them up, much to Charlie's delight.

All the boys from 6 to 14 were taught in the same large classroom with dozens of rows of wooden desks. At six-o-clock in the morning Charlie had one hour to wash, dress, make his bed, clean his shoes and say his prayers before going outside for 45 minutes of gymnastics and then breakfast of bread with porridge. Morning classes started at nine for three hours with no break and the same in the afternoon.

Morning Classes.

9 am		Historical and Bible Reading.
10 am		Arithmetic and Tables.
11 am		English Grammar and Dictation.
12 noon	Dinner	Suet Pudding with Meat, Gravy and Potatoes.
1 pm		Recreation.

Afternoon Classes.

2 pm		Writing and Arithmetic.
3 pm		Reading.
4 pm		Geography.
5 pm		Finish and recreation.
6 pm	Supper	Vegetable Broth and Oatmeal.

All meals were served in the hall on long wooden tables with all boys facing to the front. After supper, they had free time to play games and talk to each other until eight when they all, regardless of age said their prayers and retired to bed. Each Saturday the boys stacked the trestle tables to one side and sat in small groups on the hard floor where they were shown tailoring and basket making skills by visiting artisans.

Some musical lads including Abe, learned an instrument and played in a band. Each Sunday morning boys and girls from both schools marched to the Kingston Hall where they attended Sunday School in the Mission Room and then marched back again. Sunday afternoon was free time and many of the boys would go and play down by the river on the tow path. Supper was half an hour earlier on Sundays and afterwards the chaplain held extended prayers before bed at half past seven.

The chaplain was a kind man but rather weak on discipline and the bigger boys often messed about at the back of the class. Occasionally they were caught and brought to the front to have their knuckles rapped with a ruler, but most of the time they got away with it. Mr Prett, the master who taught writing and arithmetic was a different character altogether. He would patrol up and down each row of desks and any boy that was not concentrating on his work would be hit round the head with the back of his hand. One day Charlie was singled out to stand at the front next to the master's desk to recite his seven times table.

> *"One x 7 is 7, two x 7 is 14, three x 7 is 21, four x 7 is 28, five x 7 is 35, six x 7 is 42, seven x 7 is 49, eight x 7 is?"*

Charlie hesitated, Mr Prett swung round, grabbed his ear, tweaked it round and pinched hard.
> *"Open your hand Plant."*

Charlie's hand was slowly and deliberately thrashed with Mr Prett's ruler as he counted to 56. After that day Charlie always made sure he had learned his tables, dates and capital cities and never forgot that eight x 7 is 56.

The days and months passed by without much to break them up, there were no school holidays although some of the boys with families did go away for a week or so to see them. Charlie had nowhere to go. His brother Fred, had a wife and baby of his own and was struggling to make ends meet. Mercy worked seven days a week and was only allowed alternate Saturday afternoons off. Joanna regularly wrote to her sisters Sarah and Julia but she never came to Kingston and did not mention Charlie in her letters. Charlie didn't mind, he had his friend Abe.

On 6th May 1866 two days after Charlie's eleventh birthday, which passed by like all the others with no mention, Joanna married a widowed gentleman and became Mrs Chamberlain. She had left her dressmaking job and was working as a barmaid at The Albany Tavern in Great Portland Street. Mr Stephen Chamberlain, an Irish cork manufacturer, was a regular customer and had recently lost his wife. He was a charming well-dressed man living on dividends and very generous with his money. The romance between

Joanna and Mr Chamberlain flourished rapidly. Joanna was swept off her feet with expensive gifts and flattering talk and before she knew it she was married and with child. The new family started out in Lambeth, then moved to Stoke Newington shortly before Stephen was born, they had eight children in total. They moved again to the Walworth Road before eventually settling in Islington with Mr Chamberlain as landlord of The Royal William, a large public house on the Essex Road, a veritable gin palace. It seems his dividends had dried up or been spent and he was having to work in the trade he loved as a licenced victualler.

Charlie and Abe continued with their double act to entertain their pals. Abe was now very adept with a penny whistle and also a member of the church band that marched at the head of the school parade on high days and holidays. The summer was coming to an end and Master Abraham Thomas had reached the age of fourteen, it was time for him to join the merchant navy as a ships' apprentice like his father before him and Charlie's brother James. Charlie had talked of his brother to Abe and was worried when Abe told him he was off to sea. Abe laughed, Charlie's concern did not put him off, he relished the prospect of adventure on the high seas although he would miss his good friend, he promised to write from every port. Charlie had no desire for adventure and was sad to lose his best friend in the world. He took over the role of telling tales to the younger boys and added a few of his own. He had little memory of the stories his sister Mercy had told about his great grandfather the wealthy miller in Norfolk but some of his tales were about millers or mariners.

What Charlie did not know was that his brother James had returned from New York in rather mysterious circumstances and was living in Westminster very close to where their sister Mercy was a housekeeper. James was now a porter in an upholstery workshop and his foreman had a lovely daughter called Amelia who was just seventeen. They married on Christmas Day 1867 with the blessing of Amelia's father. Mercy attended their wedding but no one told Charlie, he always thought his brother stayed in America.

Charlie was now twelve and really enjoyed his Saturday classes with a cheerful old gentleman called Benjamin Wells, a basketmaker from Town End, only a short walk up river along the tow path. Mr Wells supplemented his income once a week by sharing his skills at the boys' school for the price of 1/6d. Charlie was an eager student and a quick learner just like his own boy Daniel. This encouraged Mr Wells to be more adventurous. There was much to learn: randing, slewing, fitching, cross fitching, staking, upsetting and waling were the techniques touched upon, but only practise would allow Charlie to master the craft. While they were working sitting cross legged on the hard floor Mr Wells described where he lived and how he prepared the willow rods along with his son Daniel who was 14 and already a skilled basket maker. Charlie thought how good that must be to work with your father and have a family to go home to.

In 1869 Charlie's sister Sarah reached full age of 21 and her fixed term in the school laundry was at an end. Sarah did not like the work and decided to make her own way by finding lodgings in Wood Street at the same place where she had stayed with her sister Mercy a couple of years earlier, The Two Brewers. Miss Neale was no longer there and the new landlady was not as particular. It was a rough place but cheap and Sarah was not very well. She had worked long and hard in the damp school laundry and it had affected her chest badly, she was suffering from consumption and had a persistent cough. Mr Harmsworth was notified and as her guardian summoned Sarah to his office. He explained that she was now responsible for Julia and Charlie and his authority had ceased. He could see that Sarah was not well and suggested that he continue to oversee her family responsibilities whilst providing her with a small income to live on from the Post Office Savings Bank.

Mr Harmsworth also suggested that Sarah should make a will with Fred as executor. Fred and Mercy had lost touch with their brother and sisters in Kingston. Fred and his wife Betsy now had three children and another on the way. They were living in Deptford and Fred was out of work. Sarah had not seen or heard from Fred since his wedding but Joanna had been writing to Sarah and Julia on a regular basis so it was agreed that Joanna, as the eldest married sister should be her executor.

When it was time for Charlie to leave school, Mr Harmsworth arranged a meeting at the Magistrates Court with Mr William Smith, a master tailor residing in Thames Street. Harmsworth had all the necessary documents including Charlie's school report:

"An intelligent hard-working boy with a particular talent for handicraft."

Mr Smith asked to meet the boy and Charlie was sent for immediately. James Harmsworth J.P. was anxious to place Charlie and could not praise his virtues highly enough. Mr Smith was an astute man and on meeting Charlie who was dressed in his Sunday best, agreed there and then to the apprenticeship terms. Two documents were signed by Mr Smith, one was witnessed by Harmsworth and his colleague the town bailiff, the other by the apprentice overseer who was responsible for checking the welfare of his charge at six monthly intervals. This document was given to Charlie and immediately whisked away by Mr Harmsworth to keep with his records at the solicitor's office. Master Charles Plant was now tyed to Mr William Smith as an apprentice linen draper until he became of full age.

Chapter VIII

W. Smith & Sons, Linen Drapers. Thames Street.

It was Wednesday the 5th May 1869, the day after Charlie's fourteenth birthday. He was taken back to school and told to pack his things and say goodbye to his friends. The overseer, whose name remains a mystery walked with Charlie to Thames Street, a busy narrow thoroughfare leading from the market place. The overseer shook Mr Smith's hand and nodded to Charlie. His new master introduced his two sons and Fred, the youngest, took Charlie to his room over the back of the shop that they were to share. Charlie had never had so much luxury, his own bed, a chair and a small cupboard to keep his belongings.

Mr William Smith was a tailor of good repute, a widower nearing the age of retirement who had taught his sons Will and Fred the craft of tailoring, but neither of them took to it. Their father agreed that they should take over his shop and become linen drapers. Will, his eldest son wanted to specialise in Manchester goods exactly as Charlie's father had done thirty years earlier. They purchased bolts of calico, cotton, linen and flannel, along with a selection of household long-cloths, Irish linen handkerchiefs, tablecloths, serviettes, blankets and towelling. Will had recently married Miss Caroline, the daughter of a draper and they shared the front bedroom upstairs with their baby daughter Louisa. Caroline had grown up in the trade and encouraged her husband to stock some more feminine items for the shop such as fine trims, lace and fancy buttons which were displayed in a prominent place by the window for passer's by to peruse.

The shop was thriving when Charlie arrived and he was eager to learn. He was given simple tasks to start with and Mr William was a good teacher. He knew Charlie had been taught some tailoring at school and talked to him about the quality of cloth and thread and their different purposes. His favourite maxim was:

> *"Know something about everything, and everything about something."*

Will and Fred on the other hand were rather impatient characters and expected Charlie to just know everything. There was a great deal of carrying, lifting, packing, unpacking, tying and labelling involved in his work as a junior apprentice. Charlie's favourite duty was to deliver goods to local customers in the town. He would be sent off with a parcel, name, address and directions and told how long it should take for him to return. Charlie loved mingling with the Kingston crowds and finding places he had never

seen before. Sometimes if he delivered the parcel to a big house, one of the servants might give him a penny for his trouble.

Fred was seventeen and with Charlie's arrival had been upgraded to junior assistant. Fred was front of house, serving the customers, cutting cloth and sorting the stock. His brother Will at 24 was the manager and he sat in a small glass booth at the rear of the shop where he carried out all the clerical and financial duties necessary to run a successful retail establishment. Will's wife Caroline, was with child again and it was going to be quite crowded upstairs but Charlie liked being with the family, it made him very happy to hear little Louisa laughing and chattering with her mother and Caroline found Charlie to be a kind and caring lad.

Charlie was looking forward to Christmas Day in 1869, he had never been with his own family on that day and now the Smiths were his family. Mr William, had retired and was living in a cottage at Seething Wells with a good view of the river. He had ordered a goose from the market which Charlie was instructed to collect on Christmas Eve. Caroline had been busy preparing plum pudding and sweetmeats for several weeks. Charlie had not forgotten his basket making skills and made a rattle for baby Louisa and small baskets for Caroline and Mr William. Will had stocked up with port wine and Fred (with Charlie's help) placed a large fir tree in the shop window on Christmas Eve and decorated it with candles and lace handkerchiefs. They moved the shop furniture around and laid an extravagant table with all their best linens and glassware. On Christmas morning Mr William, Will, Caroline, Fred, Charlie and baby Louisa sat down to the grandest luncheon Charlie had ever had. After lunch they played consequences and each did their party piece. Charlie danced a jig, this reminded him of Abe and he wondered where he might be.

Sunday the 26th December brought rain and sleet and while Will, Caroline and baby Louisa went to church Fred and Charlie set about getting the shop back to normal ready for opening on Monday morning. January and February offered miserable weather and there were not many customers out and about. On Louisa's birthday Caroline decided to take her for a walk along the river to feed the ducks. It had been raining heavily and the tow path was muddy and slippery. There were a few watermen going about their business and some ragged children playing hopscotch. Two nannies were chatting while walking their charges in perambulators along the riverside when Caroline, busy making sure Louisa did not slip, in her haste slipped herself, falling heavily onto her left side. The two nurses heard her cry out and rushed over, scooped up Louisa, helped Caroline to her feet and sat her down on a nearby bench. She pleaded for someone to fetch Mr Will Smith from the linen drapers in Thames Street just a few yards away and they dispatched one of the children.

Caroline was suffering sharp pains and when Will arrived they were getting stronger. He walked his wife very slowly back to the shop and helped her upstairs onto the bed. Charlie was sent to fetch the doctor from the High Street. He was not at home, his housekeeper said she would send him presently when he had finished his rounds. Will called their neighbour Mrs Baker, an elderly lady who was experienced in these matters. She asked for sheets, towels, boiling water and a knife and dismissed him forthwith. Caroline struggled for several hours but the baby would not come. Will was pacing the floor downstairs in the parlour. Mr William had been called to calm him while Fred and Charlie kept the shop open. When the doctor arrived, Caroline had slipped into a deep sleep and the baby was still not showing, there was nothing he could do. He went downstairs and told Will the bad news and suggested he call the curate who came within the hour but Miss Caroline died before he arrived. An inquest was held two days later by Mr Harmsworth as acting coroner, he sent his condolences to Will and hoped that Master Plant was applying himself to his work.

After Miss Caroline's funeral, baby Louisa went to stay with her grandfather at his cottage in Seething Wells. Will was not coping with his daily duties and his father suggested that Louisa would be best away from the shop. Caroline had left a large sum of money to her husband to ensure that Louisa was well looked after. Mr William found a housekeeper and nursemaid to look after him and his granddaughter in his comfortable cottage. Charlie was so sad again, he missed baby Louisa and resolved to visit Mr William and Louisa on his days off.

Meanwhile Mr Bentall a young draper from Clarence Street was proving to be quite the entrepreneur. He had opened his shop in 1867 with almost no experience at a time when draper's shops were two a penny. Clarence Street was a wide modern thoroughfare at the end of Thames Street and gaining a reputation for presenting smart modern shops where fashionable ladies and gentlemen could promenade away from the bustle of the ancient market that was narrow and cramped. Peter Robinson, where Fred Plant had apprenticed was now a department store selling all manner of items. Mr John Lewis, a previous colleague of Fred's, had opened his new drapery in Oxford Street three years earlier and Mr Frank Bentall watched its progress with interest. Their philosophy was: if the market demanded it, they would supply it and their customers loved it. It was not long before Bentall's was selling not only household and personal drapery goods but also ready-made clothing, luggage and hardware, a one stop shop for loyal clientele.

Now that Mr William was responsible for his granddaughter he visited W. Smith & Sons at least once a week. He had long private talks with his elder son Will while Fred the younger was left in charge who allowed Charlie to do some of his work. Charlie was good with the customers, they liked his cheery personality and he was always very thorough in attending to them. Fred was more than happy to let Charlie cover and in Will's absence sometimes sneaked off to The Crown and Thistle on the corner of Thames and Clarence Street to meet with his pals and play cards. Mr William was worried about his sons and wrote to his sister in law in Cheltenham to find a suitable housekeeper for them. Jane Gwinnell, their cousin, who was a similar age to Will, arrived in May and moved in to Mr William's old room. Jane was a motherly girl and a very thorough housekeeper, she enjoyed her work and was an extremely good cook.

The summer passed by much as many others, except for one special day when the Kingston Corporation announced that the turnpike on Kingston Bridge was going to be removed. There were great celebrations in Kingston and Hampton, the locals could now cross the bridge with their goods and chattels at no charge. Charlie and Fred were given the day off to join the crowds on the bridge. There was dancing on the common at Hampton Wick where the wooden gates were unceremoniously burned on a huge bonfire. While Charlie was watching the flames rise into the darkening sky he felt a tap on his shoulder and was pleased to see his sister Julia. They exchanged hugs and briefly discussed Sarah, they were both worried about her health but there was not much either of them could do to help.

Julia looked exhausted, she had been promoted to ironing which was hot and heavy work. She worked with two other girls, they would take turns to heat the flat irons on the gas range, wet the muslins and steam press assorted cotton and linen garments. This was skilled work with a proliferation of pin tucks, gathers and pleats, any creases in the wrong place were returned and the charge was docked off their wages. If an item was scalded they had to pay for repair or replacement, the matron would only accept perfection. Charlie introduced Julia to Fred and told her he was enjoying his work and that he was happy living with the Smith family. Julia then re-joined her friends from the laundry and the crowds watched a grand firework display organised by the corporation which delighted and amazed young and old alike. The atmosphere was happy and carefree and Fred and Charlie walked back to Thames Street in light hearted mood at the very end of the evening, well after eleven o clock.

Throughout the winter Mr William still visited and sometimes brought Louisa who was nearly four years old. Jane would take her off to the kitchen for some sweetmeats while Mr William talked to his sons about the shop. Will had not been attentive to his paperwork, the office was untidy and muddled. Since the death of his wife he had taken to drinking in The Crown and Thistle after business closed each evening and often would not return home before everyone had retired. He always rose early and went for a long walk along the river to clear his head, ready for the working day. Sometimes

Charlie would join him but they always walked in silence. Charlie recognised his sadness but did not presume to mention it. Christmas came and went with very little celebration, they ate an excellent luncheon cooked by Jane, but there were no games or decorations. Charlie had made little Louisa a cotton drawstring bag from the shop scrap box and Jane gave him some bonbons that she had made to put inside. Louisa was nearly four and was pleased with her bag of treasure. Mr William took her home soon after four-o-clock and Charlie walked round to Wood Street to visit his sister Sarah, while the Smith brothers opened their second bottle of port wine.

Wood Street was always busy being the rough part of town and Christmas Day was no different. The pubs were all open and the occupants had spilled out onto the narrow pavements where children were playing on the filthy cobbles among waste, drunkards and beggars. There was a great deal of shouting, laughing and drinking but no fine tables set for luncheon. Charlie entered The Two Brewers, nodded to the landlady and climbed three flights of rickety stairs to Sarah's tiny attic room. She was lying on a small iron bedstead with a straw mattress and dirty linen sheets. The casement window was wide open letting in a howling wind, along with stifling smoke from the surrounding chimneys. The room was dark, damp and bitterly cold. Sarah was pleased to see Charlie but did not attempt to rise from her bed. He asked her if she wanted the window shut but she said it was good for her chest to leave it open. She had lost weight and her clothes were damp from sweat. He had brought her some bonbons and put them on the chair beside her bed. A bowl of fowl broth was sitting on the floor untouched. Sarah told Charlie that Miss Stacy the landlady would bring her brandy and hot water before she retired and she needed nothing more. Charlie left after about an hour and walked back to the shop where Will and Fred were now quite merry, he was pleased to take some port wine with them and he thought about last year and how happy he had been on that Christmas Day.

One miserable damp Thursday in January a porter from Harmsworth Solicitors burst into the shop asking for Master Charles Plant. Fred went out to the store room and found Charlie, it was sad news, Sarah had been found dead that morning when Miss Susan Stacy had taken in her breakfast. She called the doctor who notified Mr Harmsworth and he was making burial arrangements for Friday 28th January at Bonner Hill Cemetery where Ellen was buried. Charlie was given the day off along with his sister Julia to attend the funeral. They met at the solicitor's office in West-of-Thames Street and walked to the crematorium behind the horse drawn carriage carrying Sarah's coffin, a much more appropriate ending than her mother, father and sister before her. There were a few prayers before the small gathering dispersed and went their separate ways.

Solicitor Harmsworth had possession of Sarah's will and wrote to her siblings advising them of their sister's death. Fred could not attend, he now had four children and was still out of work. Mercy was not given time off and Joanna's husband could not spare her from her duties. After the funeral Mr Harmsworth wrote another letter to Mrs Joanna Chamberlain requesting a meeting regarding Miss Sarah Plant's estate. Three days later Mr & Mrs Chamberlain arrived by pony and trap with a babe in arms and a young child, in a great flurry of activity on a crisp February afternoon. They were over one hour late, James Harmsworth disliked tardiness and kept them waiting another half hour while he attended to more important matters. In due course his clerk invited the family into his office and after the usual formalities over a glass of port the will was read.

This is the last will and testament of me, Sarah Bella Plant, spinster of the Public Schools, Richmond Road, Kingston-upon-Thames. Being of sound and disposing mind and memory at the time of this making hereof so declare it is my last will and testament revoking and making void all and every other former will or wills at any time made previously as it follows:

I give and bequeath to my dear sister Joanna Sarah Chamberlain formerly Plant all my worldly possessions all my funds invested in the Post Office Savings Bank, all my goods, chattels, clothes and personal effects. I give bestow and bequeath to my said dear sister, her executors' advisors and assign to hereby nominate, constitute and appoint my dear sister Joanna Sarah Chamberlain formerly Plant my sole executrix being perfectly confident and satisfied that my dear sister Joanna Sarah Chamberlain will share the said funds within the family as she thinks appropriate and as I would do if I had been a survivor.

Sarah Bella Plant.

The Chamberlains were delighted, they were to inherit nearly £200, enough to pay their debts with plenty left over. Joanna could not wait to tell Julia who was now of age and ready to leave the school laundry.

Mrs Chamberlain swore an oath to enable the solicitor to proceed with the probate. The Will of Sarah Bella Plant formerly of the Public Schools, Richmond Road, but late of Wood Street, Kingston-upon-Thames in the County of Surrey. Spinster who died 20th January 1871 at Wood Street was proved at the Principal Registry by Joanna Anna Chamberlain (Wife of Stephen Chamberlain) of 221 Hackney Road in the County of Middlesex the sister, the sole executrix on 6th March 1871.

Joanna wrote to Julia asking her to come and live with her family and work as a barmaid. Julia did not have to be asked twice and moved to Islington within the month. Julia visited the shop to say goodbye to Charlie on her way to the railway station and that was the last time he saw any of his brothers and sisters. He had no idea that Joanna went on to have eight children and died at the age of 44 when her youngest child was 6 years old, or that Julia stayed on at the pub and took over the care of those children and she herself died three years later. He had no idea that Fred was widowed twice with six children and went on to be a railway engineer's clerk in Deptford. He had no idea that Mercy died in Saint Georges Hospital from kidney failure when she was 48 or that James had returned to London, married twice and fathered three children. Nor did he know in 1871 that Joanna had left £20 with Harmsworth Solicitors to be kept in the Post Office Savings Bank for Charlie when he finished his apprenticeship.

Chapter IX

Trouble at W. Smith & Sons.

It was customary for the overseer to visit at six monthly intervals to check Charles Plant's progress and ensure his master was taking diligent care of the young apprentice. Charlie was happy in his work. Mr William was a good employer and the official papers could be signed and sealed. Charlie had been with the drapers now for four years and was competent in all his duties. The next stage would be to learn clerksmanship but Will was a reluctant teacher and did not like anyone interfering with his paperwork. Mr William had stepped back completely and assigned the business over to Will.

The shop was always busy but there was only a small profit on cut cloth. Charlie was managing the Manchester goods and responsible for customer orders. All fine linens and cottons were rolled out on the enormous mahogany counter that had a two yards brass ruler set into it. Measurement was taken to exactly one inch extra at each end, the selvedge was snipped and then one thread drawn along the weft to mark the cutting line. Heavy tailoring scissors were used for this purpose and the line had to be followed exactly along the grain of the fabric. Charlie enjoyed the precision of this task and then carefully folded or rolled the fabric, wrapped it in brown paper, tied it with string and neatly wrote out the label. The bolt of fabric would then be marked up with the amount of yardage left on the roll. If this proved incorrect when the roll was finished, the shortfall was taken from Charlie's wages even though he earned less than 2/- a week. There was a problem with this because Fred was not as thorough, he did not have to pay for his mistakes and Charlie would try to always double check Fred's labelling without him noticing.

Another problem was the premises and the location. The ancient building was run down with two very dilapidated empty premises adjacent to W. Smith & Sons. The shop was always busy on market days but the rest of the week it was quiet. New business was attracted to Clarence Street where Mr Bentall had tripled the size of his shop in just a few years. Healey's, a large linen drapery shop at the top end of Thames Street was next door to The Crown and Thistle. Will would look in their window every evening on the way to the pub to review their new stock. Mr Healey had three assistants including a young lady who was particularly skilled at selling small items of haberdashery, similar to those his dear wife Caroline would have chosen. This gave him an idea.

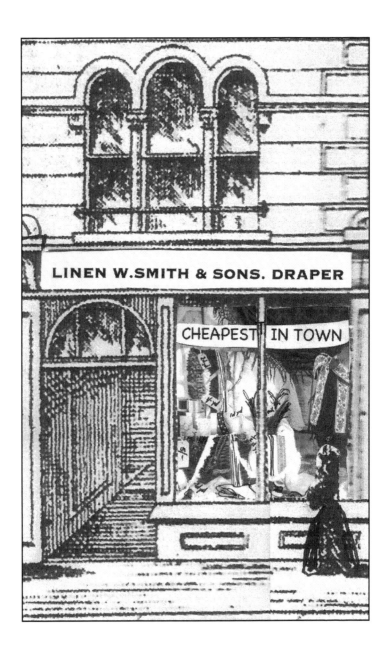

Will embarked upon a buying spree of haberdashery and ready-made items, that if he bought well would be sold quickly at double the profit of his Manchester goods. Every commercial traveller who entered the shop was welcomed and their stock rifled through with great enthusiasm to find the best items to catch the eye of ladies walking past. He instructed Fred and Charlie to empty out the window and make a large display of the new goods that he thought were fashionable and competitively priced. Charlie very much enjoyed this new duty and Fred was happy to leave him to it. Will suggested that any goods that were duplicated in Healey's should be placed in their window at a slightly lower price. He had purchased large stocks of domestic service items including aprons, cuff protectors, collars and hats, all in crisp white cotton and these were arranged on a table. Charlie added an open lidded linen basket with colourful feathers, braids, ribbons and buttons tumbling out of it. Each item had a large ticket showing the price with a handwritten sign above saying:

"CHEAPEST IN TOWN"

Market day arrived and the window brought more customers inside. News spread and the shop was generally busier, but Mr Healey, their main competitor, was not pleased. His shop was double the size of Smith's and a price war commenced. It was not long before the department stores in Clarence Street followed a similar path by offering lost leaders to attract customers into their shops. Will became obsessed with checking his prices against the other traders, determined to be the cheapest on everything and his margins dropped lower and lower until he was making no profit at all on many items. Although he had less overheads he did not have the buying power of the larger establishments and they could offer much more choice.

The rumours of Smith's cut price shop soon reached Mr William's ears and he paid a visit to find Will in his glass office with his head in his hands. His father wanted to know why he had not started training Charlie in clerksmanship and asked to look at the books. Will did not have them to hand. There were letters, invoices, catalogues, statements, bills, price tickets, labels and newspapers, all in a shambolic pile. The safe was empty, the cash box had no float and Will had no idea how much money was in it. Mr William was angry, he instructed Charlie to fetch two large boxes from the store room and they filled both of them with piles of papers. The boxes were then loaded onto a shop barrow and Charlie pushed it all the way back to Mr William's cottage, through Town End to Seething Wells where Louisa ran out to greet them. Charlie was very pleased to see her, she had grown so much and she chattered away to him like she had only seen him yesterday. They all went inside for a cup of tea and Mr William expressed his concern about the business. Charlie listened quietly and then made his way back to the shop with his head buzzing.

When he returned, the shop was shut, he knocked loudly and Jane the housekeeper came out from the kitchen to unbolt the door. Will and Fred had gone to The Crown, she raised her eyebrows in disapproval and invited Charlie into the kitchen for some refreshment. The following day business started as usual and Will set about tidying what remained of the office. He had been summoned by his father to visit the cottage with the shop books that afternoon. Will had not done any bookkeeping for over three months, he rarely went to the bank and he had been using cash from the safe to pay for his drinking. Soon after four-o-clock he arrived at his father's house who had delved enough into the paperwork to see that the financial situation was not good. There were dozens of unpaid bills. Many customers had bought items on credit but the tally book had not been kept up to date. Will had been buying goods from commercial travellers for cash but not kept a record of what he was spending. He had not checked his expenses or calculated a profit margin and was purely driven by selling cheaper than everyone else, regardless of what the goods had cost. There was a strong chance that W. Smith & Sons could be insolvent within a few weeks.

Mr William was very disappointed with both his sons who had neglected their responsibilities and fallen in with a bad crowd at The Crown and Thistle. He was an old man and did not welcome this extra burden at his time of life but he gritted his teeth and set about trying to put things right. He made a list of debts, Will, Fred and Charlie did a stock take, and a meeting was arranged with Mr Shrubsole at the bank. The Shrubsole family owned the bank as well as many commercial and private properties in Kingston including William Smith's shop. The two men had developed a good business relationship over many years and quickly agreed the shop must close down as soon as possible.

Mr William then visited his friend and colleague Mr Healey, they had known each other a long time and had a lot to talk about. They discussed the trials and tribulations of business and family life. Mr Healey had much respect for William Smith and was sorry that his sons had let him down, but was delighted to offer a knock down price for all the remaining stock which Mr William duly accepted. The figure was not enough to clear Will and Fred's debts and the tally book was beyond rescue but it went more than halfway and to prevent both his sons from becoming bankrupts, Mr William paid the shortfall to Henry Shrubsole and settled the account. Will and Fred were now clear of debt but unemployed and homeless. They went to The Crown to plan their future. Jane moved back home to her family in Cheltenham but where did that leave Charlie?

Mr William suggested to Charlie that he could lodge with him and little Louisa as a temporary measure. They notified the overseer and a meeting was arranged with Mr Harmsworth. This time Mr William went along with Charlie to discuss his future choices with the solicitor. The apprenticeship had another two years to run and Mr William was duty bound. There were no vacancies for an apprentice draper in Kingston, the old skills were dying. Female shop assistants were ten a penny, very popular with the clientele and cheap to employ.

It was suggested that Charlie could visit his brother Fred, or sister Mercy, but Charlie wanted to stay in Kingston where he had grown up. He knew the Smith family much better than he knew his own. Mr William remembered the baskets Charlie had made at Christmastide. There was a thriving basket making industry in Kingston with extensive osier beds (coppiced willow) spreading across the Hogsmill marshes and perhaps Charlie could brush up his skills learned from Mr Wells when he was at school. They all parted company having agreed that Charlie should remain lodging with Mr William while the overseer and Mr Harmsworth made some enquiries.

Chapter X

A Fresh Start With New Friends.

The overseer made his first port of call to Mr Benjamin Wells who was still teaching at the Public School every Saturday. His son Daniel was now an experienced basket maker and his younger son Albert was attending the school as a day scholar. Mr Wells remembered Charlie very well as a quiet, hardworking boy with a flair for basketry. It was nearly the end of May and Benjamin was confident that some work could be found for a fit lad of nineteen for a few weeks at the osier beds by the Hogsmill. Casual labour was taken on each spring and Daniel was currently employed as a stripper. His job was to prepare the pitted osier rods that were cut in the autumn and soaked all winter. The bark was peeled, checked for knots and branches and then laid out in the sun for bleaching. Benjamin knew the farm bailiff very well and was sure Charlie would be taken on as a day rate labourer.

The Hogsmill River is a tributary of the Thames and flows upstream from the centre of Kingston in a south easterly direction past the Guildhall, along the low flood plains due east of the town and on through Bonner Hill, Norbiton, Surbiton, Tolworth and Worcester Park. The osier beds were widespread along the flood plain, the loamy soil was perfect for growing willow. The main crop was Salix Alba, a white willow that was coppiced and provided high quality rods for making wet washing baskets and baby cribs. White willow was prized for this purpose because it did not stain or transfer any colour to the wet clothes or infant garments and linens. The trees were coppiced in November when the sap was down and the leaves had fallen. The cut rods were called withies and soaked in shallow water pits until the spring when the stripping process commenced.

The Wells family lived in Oaklea Passage, a few yards from the river at Town End. This was only a short walk from Charlie's lodgings and Mr Benjamin suggested that Charlie came around to meet Daniel and the rest of his family. Mrs Wells, a small, frail lady, wearing a simple cotton dress was sitting in the back yard on an upturned barrel with her three daughters cross legged on the ground beside her, all plaiting straw. Mr Benjamin took Charlie upstairs to the workshop where his sons, Daniel and Albert also slept. Daniel was keen to show Charlie the baskets they had made, ready for the wholesaler who came to the mill once a month to purchase raw willow bolts and readymade baskets for the London market.

The house was in poor repair, the owners were the Gray family who had previously lived in South Lane just around the corner. The area was a jumble of maltings, gravel pits and shabby houses built on marsh land. Their grandfather had purchased several plots in the demesne (old manorial land) from the Municipal Corporation in 1808 when the council were forced to raise money to fund new buildings for the accommodation of a handful of High Court Judges who were booked to oversee an important case at the County Court. They had refused to attend previously because the lodgings were not up to scratch. The gravel pits, purchased by The Lambeth Water Company were in disuse now that the reservoirs were finished at Seething Wells. Mr Sam Gray, the eldest grandson, had a philanthropic nature and was working with the town council on an extensive programme to improve the area, but the project was fraught with complications resulting in years of delays. He was a fair employer and landlord who had great respect for the working man, as did his grandfather, Samuel the elder, a self-made man who could not read or write.

Mr Benjamin was delighted to tell Charlie that the farm bailiff was willing to take him on for 1/- a day and he could start tomorrow. This was good news indeed, Charlie arranged to meet Daniel at six the following morning at the end of Oaklea Passage and together they walked to the marshes on Villiers Road, about one mile east of the town on the south bank of the Hogsmill. On arrival Charlie was led to a group of men clustered round a small wagon loaded with a variety of agricultural tools. Charlie was given a long handle hoe and followed them into the fields where the foreman, Mr Arthur, an elderly man with a severe stoop showed him how to use his hoe. Each man had his own rhyne to weed, a shallow irrigation ditch that had been dug by hand. Charlie was expected to keep up to speed with the other labourers each side of him. He was young and fit, but outdoor labouring with experienced workers was harder than he had imagined. However, Mr Arthur was satisfied with his first day's work and told him to go to the farm bailiff along with the others to collect his shilling.

The days were long and hard, working Monday to Saturday from half past six in the morning to seven at night with two short breaks during the day for refreshment. Beer was provided by the bailiff but the men were expected to bring their own food. Charlie was always given a tasty lunch of pie with bread, cheese and sometimes fruit by Mr William's housekeeper. When the first Sunday arrived, Charlie was glad for the rest. The following week was much easier, he enjoyed working outside in the summer sunshine. The weather was kind most of the time but when it rained the rhynes filled with water and the ground became sticky and unworkable.

Charlie did not have suitable footwear and his clothes got soaked. One evening on his way home he stopped off at Powell's, a Clothier Outfitter and Draper in Thames Street and purchased some Macintosh leggings, a duck jacket and some waterproof over boots. All these items came to 4/11d, he duly paid 5/- and got a penny change. Mr Powell heard his assistant talking to Charlie and joined them for a chat sending his best regards to Mr William. Charlie walked home in good spirits and told Mr William over a hot supper of his conversation with Mr Powell.

Most days Daniel and Charlie walked to work together. Daniel told Charlie about his family, how they all lived in one room downstairs where his parents and sisters also slept and that his mother was not in good health. He explained that they shared their kitchen with a newly married couple who had a young baby and rented one upstairs room next to Mr Benjamin's workshop. How water was collected from the pump in the back yard and this was shared with all the houses and their residents along with two privies (toilets) that emptied straight into the river. Charlie explained that he came from Romford and talked of his little sister Ellen who died soon after they arrived in Kingston. He told Daniel how kind Mr Benjamin and Mr William had been to him and how lucky he felt to have new family and friends. They also discussed the craft of basket making and it was agreed that Charlie should visit the Wells household every Sunday afternoon to start learning how to handle the more difficult white willow canes that Daniel and his father were now very skilled at working.

Before Charlie knew it, August had arrived and his labouring work was no longer required. The weeds were dormant and the osiers were growing tall and covered in leaf. Daniel's work was also done. The withies were dry, stacked into bolts of twelve inches diameter, thirty-two inches circumference at the butt end and graded into uniform lengths varying from three feet to nine feet. Each bolt was tied using two rods and a bond and they were stored in a dry cool dark barn ready for selling. This willow was the best quality and highly sought after by many London artisans who belonged to the Worshipful Company of Basketmakers. Now it was time for Charlie to join Daniel and Mr Benjamin full time in their workshop to improve the skills he was beginning to master. They were all employed on a piece work basis and although Charlie had managed to save some cash, he urgently needed to make some baskets to earn his living. Mr William was very kind but soon Charlie would have to pay for his own lodgings, his apprenticeship term was due to end on 4th May 1876, less than two years away, when he reached the full age of twenty-one.

The following weekend was a new holiday, Saint Lubbocks Day, a national bank holiday on Monday 7th August. The train company had laid on special cheap day returns to Brighton but neither Charlie nor Daniel could afford the fare. Instead they made their way down to the Thames and walked along the riverside downstream to Kingston bridge and beyond, watching the frantic activity as they went. It was a sunny day and the river was alive with steamers taking the rich people up river to Taggs Island and Hampton Court.

There were steamboats, punts, wherries and canoes of every imaginable size, full of gentlemen with ladies in fine hats, being rowed back and forth, upstream and downstream. The lightermen and watermen were sitting on their tethered barges with tankards of beer, smoking their pipes and watching the world go by. The two lads arrived at Turks Boatyard where Mr Turk, a keen rowing man himself was seeing off members of the Royal Canoeing Club. They were about to embark on a short race downstream to Richmond Bridge and back. Charlie and Daniel stopped to watch and enjoy the spectacle.

After the rowers had departed the two young men were just thinking about going for a drink when a deep voice shouted out:

"*Hey, Dan Wells, come over here and introduce me to your friend.*"

They turned around to see a tall man with a mass of black curly hair, waving, with tankard in hand and beckoning them over to the very last boat on the wharf. It was a dumb barge fully loaded with coal and had arrived two days earlier from the Surrey Docks. It had been towed by steam tug boat which was much quicker than using the shire horses along the tow path. The voice belonged to Sam Gray, he had been checking out the coal stocks and was partaking of a friendly drink with the bargee. Daniel introduced Charlie Plant, who Sam insisted on calling Chas and they passed a pleasant hour catching up on family news and discussing the state of the country. Sam knew Dan and his family as tenants and old neighbours and was always pleased to see him. Sam and his wife had never been blessed with children but he valued his large extended family and friends, many of whom were meeting later at The Coconut Inn in Mill Street. Chas and Dan were invited.

Charlie was delighted to be included and they both agreed to walk straight there. On the way Daniel filled him in on the Gray family who had resided in Kingston for many generations and were well known and more importantly, well liked and respected, particularly by the riverside folk. On arrival at The Coconut Inn crowds of customers were enjoying the warm evening sunshine. Dan and Charlie went inside to a private room up some steep rickety stairs to find the Gray family and friends sitting around a large trestle table weighed down with cold meats, cheeses and all manner of preserves, breads and cakes along with several large jugs of ale. Mrs Gray was delighted to see Dan, wanted to meet Chas and introduced them both to everyone. Chas was seated next to Alice, a buxom young lady with long dark hair and hazel eyes. She was the daughter of Sam Gray's cousin Henry and pointed him out sitting with her mother Emily Gray, a midwife.

Sam arrived about an hour later and insisted that the dancing should begin there and then, giving Chas a wink as he passed. Sam took his wife's hand and nodded to the fiddler to start playing. Dan was quick to rise and ask Alice's sister Ellen to dance but Charlie was reluctant, he had never danced in mixed company before and wanted to stay talking to Alice. Alice didn't mind, she liked Charlie and was rather shy herself about dancing. Shortly before midnight it was time for everyone to make their way home. Alice rejoined her family and Chas walked back with Dan to their respective dwellings all in ebullient mood.

Chapter XI

The Business of Basket Making.

It was time for Chas to settle down to hard work, Mr Benjamin recited a list of tools for him to purchase from the ironmongers in Heathen Street.

Shears:	*Strong pincers with long legs and short blades.*
Pricking knife:	*Specialist knife of rather curious shape.*
Sharp knife:	*Plain blade shaped like a razor.*
Cleave:	*Three skein cleave to split the rods.*
Shave:	*Wooden block with an inside blade rather like a plane.*
Upright:	*Block with blades for drawing skeins and trimming.*
Bodkins:	*One long round pointed, one short round pointed.*
Iron:	*For driving the work close.*
Commander:	*Iron rod with 2 teeth one end and ring at the other.*

Mr Benjamin added that the ironmonger might call this a dog.

Chas had no idea how much all this was going to cost and asked Mr William for advice. It was agreed that he should take two gold sovereigns and tell the proprietor that he had been sent by Mr Wells to purchase the items. Charlie returned with a little change from a sovereign and when he arrived home he placed the remaining gold coin in a savings tin under his bed. He kept the small change to pay Mr Benjamin for the willow rods he was going to use. His first task in his new job was the making of a yard stick from a willow wand. Each measure of one inch was checked precisely by Chas and then by Mr Benjamin and marked with a cut with his new sharp knife, the rod was cut to exactly thirty-six inches. The tool box was now complete and work started in earnest. All three craftsmen sat on the floor on a wooden ramp to support the basket which was anchored to the ramp with a bodkin.

Both Mr Benjamin and Dan specialised in oval laundry baskets for wet washing and had their own particular design. Chas had watched them and helped prepare the willow over the few Sunday afternoons when he started working with them. He was keen to progress and make the oval based laundry baskets with slanted sides that fetched good money when the London buyer came to town. The first part to be made was the oval bottom which required long and short sticks. Three long sticks together made the slath to determine the length and strength of the oval base. This was then threaded through several cleave split short sticks making an oval grid with a warp and a weft. The long slath was then bound between the short sticks and tied off to create a strong framework for the weaving. Once the base was the right size and shape the weave was interrupted with stakes to create the sides. The stakes were then pricked up with the pricking knife to make them stand upright. Next, the upsetting and byestaking in order to finish the edge of the base with a three rod waling or twining weave to provide a strong and stable edge to the base of the basket.

The next part was the most difficult, the randing weave tensioned the upsets and it was essential in Mr Benjamin and Dan's opinion that the angle remained constant throughout. Three different rod thicknesses were used, small, middle and great, to create an even, graduated stripe on the basket side that leaned outwards as it rose to the top. The slant was regularly checked by Chas, then Mr Benjamin measured and observed it at all points. Many a time Chas was told to unpick his randing to correct the tension, an irregular slant greatly reduced the value of the basket. Finally, the top border was worked with a foursome plait, making a broad and rather pleasing border capable of standing a considerable amount of wear and tear. Chas had made his first laundry basket that could be sold, it had taken him nearly three days and he may get 4/- for it from the wholesaler less 6d for the cost of materials. He was feeling very pleased with himself.

Mr Benjamin and Dan could make a basket in a day, albeit a ten-hour day. They started work at seven in the morning and worked until dark most days. The precise work needed good light but the randing and slewing could be done by candlelight. It was still summer and the best time for productivity. They were pleased to have Chas working with them, he was cheerful and a quick learner, they enjoyed his company. Dan aimed to earn at least 3/6d a day working out to threepence halfpenny an hour. Chas was currently earning half that and then only if he sold his baskets, just one penny and three farthings an hour. However, he was improving all the time and very fortunate in that he was still lodging with Mr William at no cost. Chas felt that he was a wealthy man and relished adding more cash to his savings tin after his first month's sales at the end of August with the London wholesaler. He sold five baskets for four shillings each, he paid Mr Benjamin 2/6d and put 17/6d in his tin.

Chas improved week on week and at the end of September the wholesaler bought seven of his baskets. One was rejected because the base was not flat enough so Chas took that home to Mr William's housekeeper, she was delighted with her new wet washing basket and gave him a big kiss. As the autumn set in, it became more difficult to work. The only warmth came from the small cast iron flue that rose from the kitchen range. Candles were expensive and only used when complete darkness descended on the west facing room. The tiny window gave a glimpse of sunset over the river, but most days the sun did not shine. November was cold and wet with drizzly sleet that seemed to go on forever, everything in the workshop became damp and it was difficult to keep the osier rods dry. Chas was still improving and when they all took their wares to the wholesaler at the end of the month all his baskets were accepted. He had made twelve and received £2 8s 0d and after giving Mr Benjamin six shillings, he thought he was a rich man.

The winter gave little to break the monotony of the dark damp days. Chas would meet Alice occasionally on a Sunday afternoon and sometimes he was invited to tea with her family. Mr William ordered a goose for Christmas Day and Charlie played games with Louisa after luncheon while Mr William napped in his chair by the fire. January and February were the most difficult months to get work done but Chas was almost as fast as Mr Benjamin now and very accurate with his randing tensions. The wholesaler liked his work and bought everything he made. Chas was becoming more confident and enjoyed the company of his work mates. It was agreed that they would not labour on the osier beds in the spring but continue to make as many baskets as they could, it became a competition and Chas was determined to get up to speed with Dan, even if it meant he had to put more hours in. Soon they were both making a basket a day, six days a week and Chas was saving almost all of his earnings ready for when he became independent from Mr William in two months' time. He was now earning one guinea a week and did not know how much of that he would have to pay for board and lodgings when his apprenticeship finished.

Charlie's twenty-first birthday arrived and he was summoned to Mr Harmsworth's office along with Mr William. The apprenticeship indentures were laid out on the solicitor's desk for inspection by Charles Christopher Plant, Apprentice, and William Smith Esquire, Master. The date of completion clearly stated 4th May 1876. There were also appraisals by Mr William and Mr Benjamin giving Charlie a good report for honesty, reliability and hard work.

Mr Harmsworth then indicated there was one other matter that needed young Mr Plant's attention. Charlie was worried, he wondered if something had happened to Fred or one of his sisters. Mr Harmsworth handed him an envelope with a wax seal and instructed him to open it. Inside was a statement from the Post Office Savings Bank in the name of Charles Christopher Plant with a total value of £23 14s 8d. Charlie was confused and looked to the solicitor for clarification. Mr Harmsworth explained it was his money that had been invested on instruction from his sister Joanna, when Sarah died. The account had accrued interest and was his, to do with as he wished, now that he had reached full age. Charlie was very surprised and excited, he was now even richer than he thought, he could make some plans and hoped that Mr William would advise him.

Chapter XII

Derby Day & Several Proposals.

The first thing Charlie thought was to buy Alice a present for her birthday, it was only eight days away on the 12th May when she would be twenty years old. He visited the confectioners in Thames Street that afternoon and was advised by the assistant to choose a luxury tin of Cadbury's Chocolates, a new product that was very popular with young ladies. Alice and Chas were walking out together and saw each other most Sundays. In warm weather they would meet on Queens Promenade and stroll along the river mingling with the grand ladies and gentlemen. If the weather was inclement Chas walked the one and a half miles to Alice's house where he was always given a fine welcome. Alice was the eldest of six children and helped her mother at 2 Vine Cottages in Browns Road, Surbiton. She was exactly one year younger than Chas but old for her years. Her father Henry worked at William Allen's brickworks in Red Lion Lane, but he was not in good health and had been laid off as a permanent worker. He was now a casual labourer in the summer months when he was well enough. Alice's mother Emily was a midwife and often called out at all hours of the day and night. Her youngest brother Harry was only four and Alice was expected to look after him and do the cooking. She was a particularly good cook and had a very sweet tooth.

Charlie's second task was to discuss his future with Mr William, they both sat down at the large table in the parlour with his savings tin, the Post Office statement, quill pen, paper, ink and each had a glass of port wine. The contents of the savings tin were tipped out and counted by Charlie, the result of two years savings amounted to a cash total of £62 17s 6d, this added to his Post Office Savings totalled £86 12s 2d, a veritable fortune in Charlie's eyes. Mr William thought it would be wise for Charlie to pay £60 into the Post Office where it would be safe and accrue interest. The remaining £2 17s 6d (about two weeks wages) could be kept in his tin for unforeseen expenses. Mr William suggested if Charlie wanted to stay as his lodger, his weekly rent should amount to one days' work, in other words 3/6d. Charlie readily agreed. Mr William was delighted, he liked having Charlie about the place and had a fatherly affection for him. His granddaughter Louisa was now at boarding school, his sons had moved away and were not good correspondents, he enjoyed the company.

Charlie had already told Mr William of his feelings for Alice and asked his advice on "getting wed". Mr William was very pleased that he had found romance, but thought it prudent to wait a few months as Alice was still not of full age. They had the summer before them and should take the opportunity to enjoy themselves a little before settling down. He pointed out that marriage brings responsibility and should not be rushed into. Chas heeded Mr William's words and thought about all the things he and Alice could do now that he had some money to spend. It was agreed that he should pay ten shillings a week into his Post Office savings and the matter of marriage would be discussed again in six months' time. Mr William suggested that Chas could take Alice to The Epsom Races at the end of the month. Chas thought this a very good idea and would tell Alice on her birthday. Alice was thrilled with the chocolates and very excited at the prospect of going to the races. Chas told her about his inheritance and that Mr William wanted him to stay on as a lodger, all was looking very rosy and they were both blissfully happy.

Wednesday 31st May arrived and Chas made sure he was at Browns Road to meet Alice at eight in the morning with money in his pocket, ready for the long walk to Epsom. Alice had risen early to prepare the picnic and was waiting eagerly at the front door, Ellen was coming too and they were meeting their cousins on the way. They set off down Surbiton Hill towards Tolworth and after about twenty minutes the road had swelled with people and carts all walking in the same direction. By the time they got to Ewell village the road was heavily congested with all manner of vehicles, horses and hundreds of people. Alice had arranged to meet her cousin, Ed Gray at The Star Beerhouse about half past nine and they arrived shortly beforehand. Ed was already there with a group of lads and lasses drinking ale and once Chas, Alice and Ellen had refreshed themselves they all continued on their way. They arrived in Epsom town amongst huge crowds further swelled by passengers from the Derby Specials, trains arriving from London and Brighton. It was a steep walk up to The Downs, the road was lined with gypsies and hawkers selling good luck charms, heather and offering to read palms for a penny. The crowds were pushed aside by the horse drawn carriages and cabs driving the rich people in their top hats and fancy clothes and Chas was in awe of it all.

Chas had bought a newspaper the previous day to check the horse racing details. He asked Mr William's advice, who could not emphasise enough how important it was "to not get carried away". Mr William also explained how the betting odds worked. Chas decided to make one bet of one shilling, on one race only, the most important race of the day, The Derby Stakes. He chose the horse Kisber because he liked the name of the jockey, Charlie Maidment, the odds were 4/1 and it was second favourite. Mr William had explained that 4/1 odds to win, meant a one shilling bet would win four shillings and his shilling back.

As soon as they reached the course, Ed led Chas to a bookmaker where he placed his bet of one shilling to win on Kisber. It was now eleven-o-clock and the whole group settled down on the grass to share Alice's picnic of bread, cheese, pie and eggs, Chas tucked in and was astonished at all the raucous activity surrounding them.

Ed had been to the races many times and showed them the best things to do. There was a steam fairground with a Ferris Wheel, Helter Skelter, several Carousels and Flying Chairs. Organ music from the rides filled the air mixed with the crowd cheering and laughing and everywhere touts were selling their wares.

"Roll up, roll up. The best show in town. Only a penny a ride."

Chas bought tickets for Alice and Ellen to go on a huge Carousel with painted horses and delighted at watching their faces as they whizzed around and up and down, all at the same time. Chas then took a turn on the Test of Strength and won a coconut for Alice on the Coconut Shy. They ate candy floss and toffee apples. There were clowns, conjurers and musicians with begging caps. Alice had her fortune read by Madame Zara who told her she would marry within the year and be blessed with many children. The spectacle was so much more than Chas had imagined and he was with his true love, life could not get much better.

Ed pointed out the best place to watch the race, on the outside bend before the final straight at Tattenham Corner. They arranged to meet just before The Derby to beat the crowd. They all gathered by the fence, Chas could not believe the horses speed as they appeared in front of him and galloped around the corner along the home straight. There was a deafening roar when the race finished seconds later and the crowd started moving in a sea of activity. The clock showed five to three and The Derby Stakes runners were in the stalls ready for the off, on the biggest race of the Epsom Calendar. The crowd fell silent waiting for the starter's gun, Chas relished the anticipation. The gun shot sounded, followed by another roar from the crowd. There were fifteen horses running and the race lasted less than three minutes. Kisber and his jockey were wearing green and as they galloped around the corner Ed waved and pointed, Kisber was in fifth place. Seconds later a thunderous roar rose from the finishing line, Kisber had one by five lengths and beaten the favourite, Petrarch. Ed was wildly incoherent and it took Chas a while to register. Alice and Ellen were both jumping up and down shouting "we've won, we've won". Chas had won 5 shillings. Alice flung her arms round his neck and he swung her round and around with joy.

Ed took everyone off to buy some ale while Alice and Chas collected his winnings. There was a long queue and by the time they got back to Ed, they were all on their second jug. Chas then bought them another before the long walk home. The group were very jolly as they walked down to Epsom where Ed and the others departed to Ashtead. Chas, Alice and Ellen were buzzing with energy, the day's events had not tired them at all and they made their way through Ewell and Tolworth to Surbiton, laughing and singing as they went. Alice told Chas what the fortune teller had said and he smiled. They arrived back at Browns Road about seven-o-clock, Alice invited Chas inside so they could both tell everyone what a lovely day it had been and how lucky Chas was. He didn't stay long, he wanted to get back home before dark, Alice came to the door with him, they kissed goodbye and Chas thanked her for the best day he had ever had.

Mr William was waiting for Chas and had arranged a light supper for them both. Chas could not wait to tell him of the days' events and Mr William beamed with pleasure as Chas ate and chattered away. Mr William had one piece of advice:

> *"Your winnings were beginners luck.*
> *Only bet once, on one race, once a year, to make it special."*

Chas always remembered this and every year from then on, he bet one shilling on one horse running in The Epsom Derby. Sometimes he won, mostly he didn't, but it always brought back fond memories of Mr William and that very special day in 1876 with his beautiful Alice.

Alice and Chas enjoyed a glorious summer. He was working six days a week but did take a day off now and then when he knew Alice would be able to meet him. In June they took the ferry from Town End across to Bushy Park and visited Hampton Court Palace. They watched the Kingston Regatta in July and in August Charlie hired a wherry and rowed Alice all the way to Molesey and back, on a scorchingly hot day. They also spent a lot of time down by the river on Sunday afternoons and when September arrived Chas spoke again to his friend and advisor about the prospect of marriage. Mr William explained that Chas must formally ask Mr Henry Gray before speaking to Alice. The days were closing in and Chas was spending more time at Browns Road on a Sunday, giving him the perfect opportunity to talk to Alice's father. He broached the subject while the women were in the kitchen preparing a tea of bread and dripping. Mr Gray was expecting the question. He knew Alice was very fond of Chas and Henry recognised that Chas was a kind, hardworking lad who would look after his eldest daughter and make her happy, they both had his blessing.

Chas reported back to Mr William who produced a book of etiquette and read out the wording he should use to ask Alice to marry him. They discussed the fact that Alice was still not quite of full age but Chas was impatient and keen to make his intentions known as soon as possible. Mr William understood his sense of urgency and advised giving Alice an item of jewellery for their engagement. He still had some pieces that had belonged to his wife and would like Chas to select something. The precious box was to hand and opened to reveal three rings, a bracelet and several necklaces with some matching earrings. Chas spotted one small droplet pearl hanging on a long gold chain and thought Alice would like this necklace very much. Mr William happily gave it to him with his fondest wishes.

On Sunday the 29th October Chas trudged through the freezing rain to Browns Road in Surbiton from Seething Wells and arrived about three. The family, Mr Gray, Mrs Gray, Ellen, George, Will, Minnie and Harry were all at home gathered round the small coal fire in the parlour toasting muffins for afternoon tea. Alice had seen him walk around the corner and rushed to open the door. Chas was soaking wet and quickly removed his duck jacket and Macintosh leggings before following Alice into the parlour with his gift in hand. With great ceremony, he went down on one knee, presented Alice with a tiny silk drawstring bag and asked her if she would do him the honour of becoming his wife. Alice beamed from ear to ear, her mother rushed over, kissed her and then Chas. Mr Gray, who had already told his wife Emily, shook his hand vigorously. Ellen and Minnie were jumping up and down and the boys were all laughing. Alice opened the tiny bag and tipped out the dainty necklace, she loved it and had said YES. Chas had never been so happy in his entire life and was very pleased to be offered a hot muffin with cherry preserve in celebration.

Bonfire Night at the Market Square, Kingston-upon-Thames.

Chapter XIII

The Wedding & Other Celebrations.

The following Sunday was Bonfire Night, a big event in the municipal calendar of Kingston-upon-Thames. The pyre had been built on the Fairfield over several weeks and the Corporation were footing the bill for a spectacular firework display. Alice's Uncle Sam was involved in the planning and rallied all his friends and relations to take part in the procession. Alice was keen that Chas should join them and be a torch bearer. He was beginning to realise that marrying Alice also meant embracing her huge extended family, which made him feel warm inside. The procession was fixed to start from the Coronation Stone in the Market Place. As usual on a Sunday, Chas had walked to Browns Road for the afternoon and now the whole family including little Harry were walking back with him to Kingston. Their arrival in the market place at dusk was met with a loud cheer from Sam Gray who was officiating the event along with Major Macaulay, the newly appointed borough surveyor. The Gray family were called over to collect their torches and told to line up four deep behind the leaders, ready for the walk to the Fairfield.

The church bells tolled at six-o-clock and it was time to march. Sam Gray and Major Macaulay led the procession by horse and cart with a torch at each corner carrying Guy Fawkes, a larger than life scarecrow figure made of straw, dressed in a cape with a huge hat. Chas had learned about the Gunpowder Plot at school and knew that King James had decreed that all England should have a great bonfire every November on the fifth day to celebrate his survival, when the plot by the Catholics to blow up the Houses of Parliament failed. Over one hundred people joined the march lit with flaming torches for the short half mile to the Fairfield. Everyone knew the words of the chant that was sung over and over again on the way to the bonfire.

> *Remember, remember the fifth of November.*
> *Gunpowder treason and plot.*
> *We see no reason, why gunpowder treason*
> *Should ever be forgot.*
>
> *Guy Fawkes, guy, t'was his intent*
> *To blow up King and parliament.*
> *Three score barrels were laid below*
> *To prove old England's overthrow.*

*By God's mercy he was catch'd
With a darkened lantern and burning match.
So, holler boys, holler boys, let the bells ring.
Holler boys holler boys, God save the King.*

*And what shall we do with him?
Burn him!*

The cart pulled into the torch lit Fairfield and made way to the bonfire that had a tall ladder leaning against it to reach the top. The guy was eased up onto the pyre by two strong men while the crowd that had now doubled in size were yelling:

"Burn him! Burn him! Burn him! Burn him!"

Once Guy Fawkes was positioned on high, a great cheer rose from the crowd. Major Macaulay announced the fire was to be lit by the Mayor, the Honourable Henry Shrubsole J.P. who was present in all his regalia. The second great cheer arose and then again as every torch bearer in turn, including Chas, walked around the pyre and threw in their torches. The flames rose quickly on the cold crisp evening and the warmth of the fire was welcomed by the crowd.

Alice was eager to catch her uncle and tell him she was betrothed to Chas, he was delighted and shook Chas's hand very heartily.

"You are one of us now lad."

Sam had booked stall holders on behalf of the Corporation, all selling their wares for a halfpenny: pea soup, baked potatoes, hot eels, German sausages, roasted chestnuts, crumpets, plum duff and sherbet. He suggested they all get something to eat and it was his treat. There were also penny pies, ginger beer and hot wine. The Gray family were gathered in a large group tucking in to their tasty supper with Alice, Chas and Uncle Sam at the centre. Meanwhile it took about twenty minutes for the flames to reach Guy Fawkes and in a flash, he was gone, another cheer rose into the night air. Time for the fireworks which surpassed all expectation, Queen Victoria herself would have been proud of the municipal show that Royal Kingston-upon-Thames had laid on for its people.

Once November had set in Chas was working hard with Dan and Mr Benjamin to keep up to speed with his baskets. He wanted to match his summer production to enable him to keep on saving ten shillings a week in readiness for his marriage. When he told Mr Benjamin and Dan his good news they congratulated him and said what a good family he was marrying into. Meanwhile, Alice and her mother had visited the vicar at Christchurch in King Charles Road and arranged for the Banns to be read the first three Sundays in December in preparation for the wedding on Thursday the 4th January. The Reverend Barker knew Mrs Gray very well, she always attended the baptisms and sadly, also some funerals of the babies she delivered and he was looking forward to meeting young Mr Plant.

Alice's cousin Jessie was a dressmaker and lived in South Bank, the next road up from Browns Road. She had lodged and worked with their grandmother Jane Gray, a skilled seamstress who had recently died. Mrs Gray senior had taught all her daughters and granddaughters to sew, but Jessie took her talent further and was running her own business. Alice went to see Jessie to announce her news and ask if she could help her with a new dress. Jessie had recently been given a brown silk day dress by one of her customers because it was a little out of fashion. Jessie had altered it to fit herself but she had not worn it yet and Alice was welcome to borrow it. Alice's mother Emily took all three daughters on a shopping trip to Bentall's where they purchased new winter bonnets in browns and blues. Her father Henry, was a gardener and had cut some hydrangea heads back in October. They were arranged on the parlour table near the fire and had dried out nicely to a beautiful copper pink. Alice could have those for a bridal posy and Jessie gave her some blue silk ribbon to tie them with.

Unknown to Chas, Mr Benjamin was making a hedgerow bower trimmed with holly and ivy to be placed at the church entrance. Christchurch was a new building and rather austere in Mr Benjamin's opinion. The main door opened straight onto the road and Mr Benjamin thought a rustic bower would fit the occasion well. Chas was instructed by Alice to be at Browns Road on the first three Sundays in December bright and early ready for the matins service when the Banns were to be read. Chas had not thought about what he was going to wear for the wedding but Alice had; she suggested he buy himself a new shirt, and trousers. He asked Mr William's opinion and they both visited Mr Denchfield in West-of-Thames Street who was always well stocked in readymade items. Mr William was of similar stature to Chas and offered the loan of his black frock coat. Chas tried it on, it was too long in the sleeves, but Mr William soon remedied that with his tailoring skills.

The question of the ring was another matter, Dan was to be best man and he suggested the pawnbroker in Wood Street. It was a shabby rundown building with a small door opening onto the street. Inside there were piles of clothes in one corner and household items in another. The back of the shop was protected by an iron grid and an elderly gentleman wearing glasses was sitting behind it at a desk reading the newspaper. Dan knew Mr Duckett very well and acknowledged his presence.

"What can I do for you today Master Wells?"

Dan explained that his friend was getting married and wished to purchase a wedding ring. The gentleman put his newspaper down, took an enormous key out of his breast pocket and opened the door behind him. He was gone a good few minutes and returned clutching a wooden chest. This was unlocked and a small tray with about twenty rings of mixed quality and design in silver and gold, some with stones, others plain, was revealed. Chas had decided to spend no more than one guinea, and asked what he could have for that price? Mr Duckett muttered under his breath and pulled out a tiny 22 carat gold band in a beautiful rich yellow. It was worn thin with a couple of dents and the edges sharp but Chas thought it could look very well on Alice's slim finger. Dan asked if it could be less than a guinea, the pawnbroker muttered again and replied:

"As it's you Master Wells, your friend can have it for a pound."

Christmas Eve was on a Sunday in 1876 and Chas walked to Browns Road as usual in time for church which today was a Carol Service. Will and Minnie were in the Sunday School choir singing, "O Come, All Ye Faithful". The Reverend Barker gave a long sermon about the meaning of Christmas. A nativity scene stood next to the altar with very brightly painted statues of Joseph, Mary, the baby Jesus, the Wise men, Shepherds and the Angel Gabriel. Chas thought it a very nice service despite the long sermon. Unusually, the family all adjourned to The Victoria Inn after church where Henry and Chas got in the drinks for everyone, even little Harry had a small cup of ale. Henry was in deep discussion with John King, the landlord, about the wedding breakfast. Mr King assured Henry that his wife Kezia would lay on a good spread and there was no need to worry. Henry handed over ten shillings and hoped that would be sufficient, Mr King agreed. The afternoon passed with great merriment, there was much to look forward to. Chas said his goodbyes later than usual and walked back home to Seething Wells in the dark.

Mr & Mrs Gray had invited Chas for dinner on Christmas Day but he declined. He wanted to celebrate one last time with Mr William. On Christmas Eve Louisa had returned home from school for the holiday to find her grandfather setting up a tree which they both then decorated. The goose was ready for roasting on a spit in the scullery and the housekeeper had excelled herself in the preparation of many sweetmeats and delicacies. The parlour table was set with all the best glassware, china and linens just like that first Christmas seven years ago when Charlie first joined the drapers as an apprentice. On Christmas morning Chas rose to find Louisa by the fire reading and after breakfast, Mr William poured Chas a glass of port wine which he raised as a toast:

> *"Master Plant, to you and your future, may you be happy*
> *and successful in your marriage and your life."*

Chas thought of Mr William as a son would a father, he had always been very fair and kind to him. He had lost all his brothers and sisters with no memory of his own parents but he was a very lucky man with his adopted family. Luncheon was even grander than before with hot eels, pike, sweetbreads, goose with all the trimmings and baked pork followed by pineapple, cheese, plum pudding and petit fours, all washed down with an assortment of wines specially selected by Mr Willam. The meal lasted several hours and when the brandy was poured it was time to open the gifts under the tree. Louisa was given charge of this duty and Chas was surprised to receive three parcels wrapped in brown paper and string. The first, from Louisa, was a Berlin Wool embroidery with the words:

"HOME SWEET HOME"

Chas loved the very bright colours of yellow, red, blue and green, all set on a black background with the initials, L. S. age 9, stitched in the corner. Chas gave her a big hug and kissed her on the cheek, what a lovely gift that he would treasure forever. The housekeeper gave him a bag of bonbons and she was congratulated on her culinary expertise. Lastly, a small box from Mr William. Charlie opened it, and inside there were three gold stud buttons for his new shirt. He was overwhelmed with emotion and shook Mr William's hand, they both had tears in their eyes.

The remainder of the day passed with Chas and Louisa playing consequences while Mr William had a nap and later they all played cribbage. Mr William had been teaching Louisa and they let her win. Chas helped the housekeeper clear the dishes and they retired having had the very best Christmas. The following day was also a holiday but Chas had lost a few days in December and went into work to catch up. He was in the workshop on his own, Dan was at the races and Mr Benjamin was resting downstairs with his family. Chas enjoyed his solitary day of reflection.

On New Year's Eve, the Gray family, who had a smattering of Scots in them always celebrated Hogmanay. Chas was banished from Browns Road while the women cleaned the house from top to bottom in readiness for the New Year. All the coal was taken out of the grate, the curtains and rugs were beaten, the floors were polished and the range was blacked. Alice had explained about first footing and thought it would be great fun for Chas to take part. It was agreed that he should meet her father at The Victoria Inn for an evening drink and wait for the bells to toll at midnight. The family were gathered in the parlour dancing and singing songs when midnight struck. Mr Gray pressed a lump of coal into Chas's hand and ushered him out of the pub and around the corner to the cottage. He was told to knock on the door and present the coal to whoever opened it, it was of course Alice who laughed with glee, took the coal and invited him in. A dark stranger had first footed them and brought good luck to the house for the following year. The evening continued long into the early hours with singing and parlour games and they all retired to bed well after three. The next day was another holiday and only three days before the wedding, they rose a little later than usual about 8-o-clock and Chas made his way back to Seething Wells for a quiet day with Mr William; he had rather a sore head.

Thursday the 4th January arrived and Chas was up before dawn. The howling wind and heavy rain had kept him awake much of the night and he was eager to get the day started. Mr William had booked a gig from the railway station to take Chas, Dan and himself to the church. Dan arrived at the cottage in plenty of time and they all took breakfast together. Chas was not hungry but managed to eat some porridge while Dan tucked in to porridge, kippers, eggs, toast and gooseberry jam. The service was due to start at ten and Chas wanted to be there by nine to make sure all was in order. They were in their Sunday best and Mr William summoned the cab man for eight thirty. The rain was lashing down and the gig was covered in a waterproof sheet, as was the driver. They set off on time and arrived at King Charles Road in a very damp state. On entering the church, the Reverend Barker welcomed them and suggested they leave their wet clothes in the vestibule. They were the first to arrive.

Most of the guests walked to the church in the terrible weather. The pews gradually filled with friends and relations. Uncle Sam and his wife Annie Gray arrived in their gig with Mr Benjamin who had left his wife and daughters at home. The bride and her family were only five a minute walk away. Cousin Jessie and her family, the Emmetts lived even closer. Aunt Annie had loaned Alice a very stylish French parasol. Her father put a sixpence in her shoe for luck, she had her old petticoats, her new bonnet, her borrowed silk dress and blue posy ribbons. Most importantly she was wearing the pearl necklace that Chas had given her at their engagement. There were about twenty-five guests and they all sung heartily as the bride walked up the aisle in her brown silk dress and matching bonnet, with her father at her side and her sisters Ellen and Minnie following behind. Chas stood next to Alice and the service began, Dan gave Chas the ring, Charles Christopher Plant and Alice Mary Gray made their betrothal, the congregation sang: "All Things Bright and Beautiful" and then Chas, Alice, Henry and Ellen went into the vestry to sign the wedding certificate and all the guests followed.

Christchurch. King Charles Road, Surbiton, Surrey.

Alice had told the Reverend Barker that she was of full age. She was actually only twenty but would be twenty-one in four months' time and her father was present as a witness, so no matter. Her sister Ellen was excited to be part of the official proceedings as a bridesmaid and a witness. The Reverend John Barker then asked Chas for his father's full name and profession. Chas could not remember Michael Frederick Plant or perhaps he did remember and preferred to forget, he said:

"William Plant, a Draper,"

in respect to his kind and generous master, Mr William Smith, tailor and draper. The ceremony was complete and as the bride and groom left the church they walked hand in hand under the rustic bower held up proudly by the two Mr Wells. The congregation followed and threw rice over the happy couple as they ran to The Victoria Inn on the Ewell Road through the driving rain. They didn't mind getting wet, they were wed.

Chapter XIV

Married Life & Fatherhood.

The wedding breakfast was a quiet affair and all done by two-o-clock. There were no speeches, Dan and Mr Benjamin had to get back to work. The happy couple were congratulated by all the guests as they departed which just left Mr William and the Gray's. They stayed on and chatted for a while before Mr & Mrs Plant made their way back to 7 Richmond Grove, around the corner from Alice's parents. They were renting one small room and Alice could not wait to make it her own. She spent the following week with the help of Ellen and Will moving her things from Browns Road. Mr William had given Chas a few household items, including a feather mattress and some linens. The following Saturday Uncle Sam Gray arrived at Seething Wells with his horse and cart to move Chas's belongings to Richmond Grove. Sam was strong and practical, he and Chas had a good day working together and getting to know each other. That evening Chas hung Louisa's sampler over the bed, he and his wife had a home of their own and were content.

"HOME SWEET HOME"

Chas returned to work immediately and was having to leave much earlier to make the long walk to Mr Benjamin's and getting home late in the dark. Alice was still cooking for her family and although they often shared meals together Chas liked it best when just he and Alice ate supper at their small table lit with a candle in their own room. Alice was blooming and chose one of these evenings to tell Chas she was with child. His delight was unbounded, he was such a lucky man and he promised to be a good father. The spring brought longer days and some sunshine and the young couple were able to enjoy a few outings over the summer, before Mabel Emily Plant was born on the 13th October 1877, with Emily Gray in attendance as midwife.

Chas was at work and arrived home at the usual time to find Alice and their new born asleep in bed. He could not describe the joy he felt when he saw his child and the serene look on his wife's face. His baby daughter was only four hours old. A fire was burning and a candle lit the table where a cold supper was waiting for him. He ate quietly and slept on the floor that night. As soon as Chas knew he was going to be a father he started making a crib, it was more ornate than his laundry baskets and Mr Benjamin had helped him with some fancy open weaving to make it special. It was at the workshop and he would bring it home the next day for baby Mabel to settle in, they could now begin proper family life.

Chas was matching Dan in speed and quality with his basketry and they were both teaching Albert with Mr Benjamin advising. Mrs Wells had died in February from consumption and the girls were now boarding at the Richmond Road School to train as laundresses. Mr Benjamin who was nearly sixty was suffering with lumbago and had gnarled and twisted arthritic hands. On some days he could not manage the stairs to the workshop but he was still able to prepare the osier rods in the parlour and do a little basket weaving. He could not afford the doctor, but his mother, a Romany gypsy, had taught him about herbs and their medicine when he was a child. He made a poultice from black bryony leaves that grew in the hedgerow and purchased Tincture of Aconite from the apothecary for rubbing into his hands and aching back, to ease the pain.

In 1877 the rainfall again broke all previous records. The Thames was flowing high and the Hogsmill had burst its banks making it very difficult to work the osier fields thus creating a shortage of good quality white willow and the price went up from six pence to nine pence a basket. The wholesaler refused to raise his buying prices for the finished baskets and Chas was having to work extra hours to make up his loss of one shilling and sixpence a week. The weekly rent at Richmond Grove was four shillings and the biggest expense in the winter was coal and candles. Chas had not earned enough last winter to cover those costs and his savings were shrinking.

Mr Benjamin knew Chas was worried and told him of a room to rent on Fairfield South. The house was owned by Henry Shrubsole the highly respected town mayor, magistrate and businessman. The name Charles Christopher Plant was familiar to the Honourable Mr Shrubsole from his dealings with Mr Harmsworth and Mr William Smith. Chas asked Mr William to recommend him and his excellent references resulted in an offer of a short tenancy at a subsidised rate of two shillings a week. Chas suggested to Alice that if they moved to Kingston, they would save money and he could be home earlier to be with her and the baby, particularly now another cold winter was imminent, Alice reluctantly agreed.

Chas and Alice moved into a basement room on the Fairfield in November when Mabel was one month old. There was one window and a fireplace. The kitchen, with a cold tap and coal range was shared with several other tenants as was the privy at the end of the garden. Alice made friends with the Allen family who lived upstairs, they had a baby called Fred who was nearly one year older than Mabel. Chas was working longer hours but getting home sooner, it was only a short walk from Oaklea Passage just the other side of town but he was worried about his wife and baby. Mabel was sickly and

Alice missed her mother's support. Emily Gray visited as often as she could. It was a long and difficult walk on cold wet days and she discouraged Alice from going out in the damp weather.

When spring arrived both Alice and Mabel perked up a bit and once a week Alice walked to Surbiton Hill with the baby in her perambulator to visit her mother and sister. The rain continued to fall throughout the summer and their basement room was damp and dreary. Alice did her best to keep it clean and dry but it was a losing battle. When the weather was fine she took Mabel out for some fresh air but those days were few and far between. Her washing never dried properly and all their bed linen and clothes smelled musty, even in high summer. Alice did have her friend Mrs Allen with little Fred to keep her company and they sometimes chatted in the garden while Mabel watched Fred playing in the mud. In August, Fred went down with a nasty chest cold but he was still quite perky. He was a kind boy and shared his toys with Mabel, who giggled when he gave her things to play with but he also gave her his cold. She could not feed properly and was coughing badly.

Alice's mother came to administer a variety of medicines including cough powders and told Alice to keep Mabel warm by wrapping a hot stone in a cloth and placing it under the bed clothes in her cot. This was all to no avail and in one short week on the 20th September 1878 baby Mabel died from pneumonia in her mother's arms, just three weeks before her first birthday. Doctor Corbett was called out to certify the death and tried to reassure Alice that it was through no fault of her own. When Chas came home he found Alice distraught with Mabel in her arms; he did not know how to calm her. He was distressed himself, he had failed his pledge to be a good father and lost his first born. Alice walked to town and registered Mabel's death the following day with Mr Harris and a burial was arranged at Bonner Hill for the following week. A very sad group followed the tiny coffin made from rough sawn wood to the cemetery where a few words were said in the presence of Chas, Alice, her mother Emily and Uncle Sam.

The following winter was extremely cold with snow on the ground from November to April. Alice's father, Henry Gray was now very unwell, the cold weather had worsened his condition and in February 1879 he died at the young age of fifty. His lungs had filled with brick dust, built up over nearly forty years of toil at the brick yard. He and his wife were living downstairs in the tiny Georgian terraced cottage with a bed in the corner of the parlour. There were two rooms upstairs, one for their daughters and the other for their three sons. They shared the kitchen and garden with a young family who lived in the basement. Emily Gray was a strong woman and coped well after her husband's death by taking solace in her children.

Alice was deeply upset by the loss of her father and needed much consoling from Chas. She had not fully grieved for Mabel and wanted to be with her mother and sisters. Chas hated seeing Alice so unhappy and agreed they should move back to Surbiton Hill. Mrs Gray joined her daughters Ellen and Minnie in their bedroom to give Chas and Alice space in the parlour at 2 Vine Cottages, Browns Road. It was agreed they should pay the same rent of 2/- to Emily in return for Alice helping with the cooking. Uncle Sam helped them move again on a bitterly cold day in March, the icy roads were treacherous and it was a slow journey but Alice cheered up a little once she was back home with her mother and warming her hands by the fire.

Ellen also took Mr Gray's death badly and became romantically involved with a certain Mr Naish, the man from the Pru, who had brought news of a small payment to Mrs Gray from her husband's Industrial Life Insurance, that he had paid one penny a week into for the past ten years. George, their eldest son was working as a general labourer on a project with his Uncle Sam, learning many new skills and paying rent for lodging with his mother. Will had been taken on as an outdoor apprentice at Jobbins Bakery on the Ewell Road and Minnie also worked at Jobbins as a house servant, on a daily basis. Ellen was assigned to housework at home and now Alice was back they shared the cooking and care of little Harry while their mother Emily continued her midwifery and nursing duties.

Eventually the snow disappeared and the days started to warm up, by May the sun had started shining. On Chas's birthday Alice announced that she was with child again. The following day he stopped off at Mr William's on his way to work to tell him the good news. Chas was greeted by the housekeeper who looked distressed. Mr William had fallen a few days earlier and was in bed, the doctor said he had cerebral apoplexy. Chas asked if he could see him and was shocked to find him unresponsive and in a deep sleep. He took his hand and told Mr William his good news, there was no response but he hoped that Mr William knew he was there. William Smith never woke and died four days later. Chas attended another funeral at Bonner Hill this time with Louisa who had arranged a headstone for her grandfather, his sons did not attend.

On the 23rd October 1879 Florence Daisy Plant was born at 2 Vine Cottages with her grandmother attending as midwife. Alice felt safe and Florence was a big baby with a good set of lungs. Chas arrived home from work to find his second daughter and wife happy and healthy, he was pleased and relieved.

Now that Alice was a mother again with her own responsibilities more work was falling onto Ellen, her brothers were not expected to help in the house. Mr Naish, the young handsome insurance man was very attentive and they started walking out together. After a few weeks he asked Ellen to meet his mother. She lived in Wales and Albert wanted to visit near Christmas for about three weeks. Mrs Gray was a little concerned, but she liked Mr Naish and he had good prospects, so off they went. Christmas passed happily in the Gray household with baby Florence to keep the women and Chas amused. When Ellen returned the following week on the eve of New Year she introduced herself as Mrs Albert Naish. Her mother was upset not to have attended the wedding but took the news in her stride until Mr Naish explained that they had taken lodgings in Kent. This was too much for Mrs Gray and she burst into tears. Ellen tried to console her, it was not far and she would be able to visit when Albert was on his Surrey rounds.

Alice would miss her sister desperately but she had her own family to think of now. The Hogmanay proceedings commenced and Chas as the eldest male, was instructed by Mrs Gray to take Albert to The Victoria Inn as she pushed a nugget of coal into his hand. Chas and Albert had many drinks, a pleasant chat and a bit of a sing song in the rowdy atmosphere. Chas discovered that Albert's mother was a basket maker with three employees and Chas was keen to find out more. At midnight, the bell tolled and the two men walked back to Browns Road. This time Ellen opened the door and Albert Naish, her tall dark stranger had brought good luck to the house for another year.

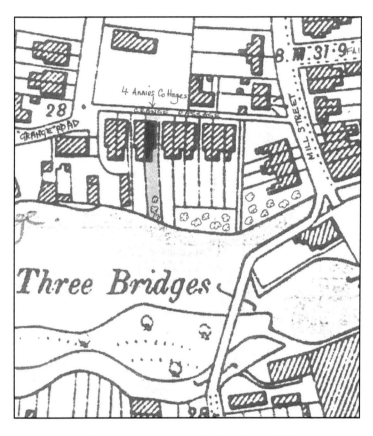

Grange Passage on the north bank of the Hogsmill River.

Chapter XV

Time to Move & Be Independent.

Chas thought a great deal about his prospects over the next few weeks. His walk to Town End had been difficult all winter, taking almost twice as long on many days due to a permanent thick fog that hung over the whole district. He was nearly run down on one occasion by a hansom cab that just appeared in front of him with no sound of hooves in the pea souper. He missed Mr William as an advisor and did not like to worry Mr Benjamin who was struggling to make ends meet and had his own troubles. Money slipped through Dan's fingers and although he worked hard he never had anything to show for it and Mr Benjamin fretted that his younger son Albert might follow the same path. Chas told Alice about Mr Naish's mother Sebrina and her basket making business in Wales. Alice liked the idea of Chas working for himself and thought it would be a good idea to talk to her Uncle Sam who knew many council officials in Kingston, most of whom were landlords.

Sam Gray was already a respected member of the community and involved in several building projects in the town. His grandfather had left him a wealthy man and he wanted to make the best of his inheritance. He understood immediately when Chas approached him about finding a house where he could live with his family and carry out his own business without responsibility to anyone else. Sam immediately thought of the new riverbank houses at Three Bridges between Avenue Road and Mill Street. Many of the osier beds had been lost to housing development, the owner had realised, like Sam, that rental from property was more profitable than farming.

There was a vacancy at 4 Annies Cottages, Grange Passage. A two up, two down, cottage with a kitchen and scullery behind, the two rooms downstairs could be leased for twelve pounds a year including shared use of the kitchen. Chas worried about the expense, but Alice was delighted and wanted to move in immediately. It was rather crowded at Browns Road now that Florrie was crawling and she wanted to see more of Chas. He took his savings book to the Post Office to withdraw the cash and the following day signed a lease in the presence of Sam Gray and his new landlord, Mr Knight.

The terraced cottage was on the north bank of the Hogsmill, the long back garden had the remains of coppiced willow growing down to the water's edge. Alice made the front room into their bedroom with a safe place for Florrie and they lived in the back parlour that opened onto a sunny yard and shared kitchen. Both rooms had gas light and a fireplace, the kitchen a cast iron range and the cold tap was in the scullery with a solid fuel water boiler for bathing and laundry. The other tenants were Annie Kelley, a widow and her daughter Mary, who were both dressmakers along with Thomas Best, a horse keeper with his wife Emily. The women gathered daily in the scullery and helped each other with laundry and cooking while Chas worked on his baskets. Annie and Mary were hardworking, kind souls but Thomas was a different character and not pleasant to his wife or his horses. Chas turned a blind eye, he had seen his kind before at school and it was best to humour Thomas, particularly when he came home worse for drink.

The summer arrived early and glorious sunshine continued through until September. The young family spent most of their time outside, working and playing with baby Florence. Chas was even able to harvest some willow and prepare his own rods. He built a small shed next to the privy for storage and stocked up with several withie bolts ready for the winter. The ground was very easy to work and Alice grew a few vegetables with herbs and pretty summer flowers to brighten up the house. Chas discovered his own gardening skills and planted potatoes and brassicas. He had watched Mr William gardening and it brought back good memories. Life continued very pleasantly, Chas was getting much more done now that he was working from home without the long walk each day. Alice and Florrie would sometimes walk to Browns Road to see Mrs Gray and catch up on all the family news. Ellen was expecting a baby and moving back to Surbiton to be near her mother who was to deliver her first born.

One beautiful sunny Sunday afternoon Alice and Chas decided to take Florrie for a walk along Queens Promenade and they bumped into Dan and Albert Wells. They had not seen each other for several months and Chas was keen to know how Mr Benjamin was. His lumbago was worse and he could no longer climb the stairs or do the basketry and was dreading the winter coming. Chas said he would go around to see him one day soon when he was in the town. The following Saturday Chas, Alice and Florrie walked to the market and while Alice shopped for meat, flour and groceries, Chas visited Mr Benjamin. He was in a very bad way, he could hardly stand and his hands were swollen and twisted with the arthritis, but he was very pleased to see Chas and offered him a chair.

They talked about Florrie and Alice and the new house with osiers in the garden. Mr Benjamin pointed to a large wooden box under the table and asked Chas to bring it to him. The contents were slowly inspected, a small trinket box, a bible, an old pair of shoes, a long sharp knife with a bone handle, two horseshoes, some baby clothes and several pieces of paper in varying degrees of decay. Mr Benjamin painfully sorted through the papers to find a large dirty parchment. It was curled at the edges and stained with watermarks but still in one piece.

"This is my Ma's recipe. I know not who wrote it."

Chas could not read it, the fancy writing was blotted and blurred but he would treasure it and thanked Mr Benjamin. He took the document home and gave it to Alice, she could not decipher it either, perhaps Uncle Sam could?

Sam Gray often called in to see Alice, Chas and baby Florrie. His brother William lived in Grange Road just around the corner and he was only a short walk away in Orchard Road. Uncle Sam and Aunt Annie did not have any children of their own but were always very keen to be involved with their dozens of nephews and nieces. Alice showed her uncle the parchment, he knew exactly who to ask. Sam Gray was not well educated, he lived on his wits, but he was sure his good friend Major Henry Macaulay would help for the price of a fine bottle of claret. Several weeks later the translation arrived written on good quality vellum in black ink and it read as follows:

The Medicinal Virtues of Willow.

Both the leaves, bark and the seed, are used to staunch bleeding of wounds, spitting of blood, and to stay vomiting, if a decoction of them in wine be drank. The leaves bruised with pepper, and drank in wine, relieves the colic. The seed has the same effect. Water gathered from the Willow, when it flowers, the bark being slit, is very good for redness of the eyes and dimness of sight. To provoke urine, if it be drank. To clear the face and skin from spots and discolourings. The flowers have the faculty of drying up humours if boiled in white wine and the liquor drunk freely. The bark has the same effect, if used in the same manner. The burnt ashes being mixed with vinegar take away warts and corns. The decoction of leaves or bark in wine takes away scurf and dandriff by washing the place with it."

Chas was delighted, he learned every word by heart and made notes in his own simple way of each instruction. He put the original parchment in his savings tin and placed the new one, in a large leather wallet where Alice kept her recipes. He wished he had known this recipe when Mabel was a baby, she vomited constantly and had cried all the time with colic. Alice's mother swore by Angelica Cordial for mother and baby, the apothecary sold very small bottles for sixpence but it did not work on Mabel. Now Chas could make up his own medicinal recipes.

The following Saturday he walked to Town End to see his old teacher and friend, Dan answered the door, Albert was there also, but no sign of Mr Benjamin. As he walked in, the cold damp air hung in the parlour, the winter was coming and Oaklea Passage sat in a permanent heavy mist rising off the river. A mixture of noxious aromas from the tannery and maltings made the atmosphere sickly to the nose. It took him back six years to when he started and realised how lucky he was to not be living or working there anymore. Dan said Mr Benjamin had admitted himself to the infirmary at Kingston Workhouse, he had been struggling with his breathing, could not work and did not want to burden his sons. Dan thought his father was receiving better care than he would at home and he was going to stay on at the house with Albert until his sisters left school. The workhouse was not a place to be visited by friends and family, Chas feared that he would not see Mr Benjamin again and went home with a heavy heart.

Chapter XVI

Annie May is Born Amongst Terrible Tragedy.

Alice saw quite a lot of her sister Ellen and baby Cuthbert. Florrie was nearly three and Cuthbert a year younger. They would all visit their mother or go to Ellen's house in Surbiton. Albert Naish was doing well as an insurance man and could afford to lease one of the new villa cottages down by Saint Matthews Church. Chas and Alice celebrated their combined birthdays with a walk to Richmond Park. They took Florrie in her perambulator and had a picnic on the grass whilst watching the deer, the fancy ladies on horseback and the gentlemen in their carriages. Alice chose this moment to tell Chas she was having another baby and thought it due around Christmastide. Chas could not stop smiling, he resolved to work even harder to support his growing family. They were just managing on his money from selling the baskets but each year he was drawing twelve pounds from his savings to pay for the lease on the cottage and the pot was getting low.

Life continued quietly for the rest of the year, Alice tired more quickly than she had with Florrie but her friend Mary Kelley from upstairs helped out with the heavy laundry. There were half a dozen houses in Grange Passage and most of them had families with children. The young widow who lived next door had two sons and her youngest, Johnnie, was the same age as Florrie. The Humphreys family lived on the other side with five children and Florrie liked playing with Mattie and Mary Fowler who lived a few doors down. Christmas came and went with no sign of the baby arriving. In January Alfie Millard, Johnnie's brother, was sent home from school with a high fever. He had a sore throat and was being sick and his mother put him straight to bed, the following day he came out in a rash all over his neck and body and his skin started peel. He had scarlatina. Johnnie went down with the same symptoms and within a few days all the children in Grange Passage were ill. Florrie was very poorly with a high fever and Alice was not getting any rest. The baby was overdue and she started getting pains in the middle of the night.

Chas called to his neighbour's window, Henry Wheatley, a bricklayer and asked if his son Harry could run to Browns Road to fetch his mother-in-law, Mrs Gray. Harry was a helpful lad and left straight away, it was pitch dark but he took a lantern to guide him along the muddy and sometimes flooded lanes and arrived at 2 Vine Cottages about two in the morning. Harry was shouting and battering the door, waking everyone in the road including Emily who knew immediately why he was there. She quickly dressed and

Chas, Alice & Florrie in Richmond Park.

put her coat on for the two mile walk back to Grange Passage. They arrived to find Alice hunched on the bed in the middle of a sharp pain. Chas was watching Florrie who had just been sick and was delirious with fever. Emily made her daughter get into bed and checked for the baby, it was a while off coming and Alice should rest. She then looked at Florrie and told Chas to bathe her brow with cold water and give her 20 drops of Tincture of Digitalis mixed with 10 drops of Antimonial Wine. Chas had these ingredients to hand for his own medicinal recipes and mixed the potion there and then.

The night seemed to go on forever for Alice and poor little Florrie but at dawn there was a sudden burst of activity and another baby girl was born. Emily gave the baby to Alice while she cut the cord and tidied up. Chas had witnessed the whole event and was beside himself with joy. Little Florrie had fallen asleep and was unaware that she had a sister. Emily went into the kitchen to boil up some medicinal wine for everyone and Chas sat on the bed with his wife and new baby. They called her Annie after the cottage where they lived and May for the month that Alice discovered she was with child.

Chas and Alice were both worried that the baby would catch scarlatina and it was agreed that Alice and Annie should go and stay with Emily until Florrie was better. That same morning Chas ran to Uncle Sam to tell him the news and ask if he could take Emily, Alice and the baby back to Browns Road in his cart while Chas stayed at home with Florrie. Chas and Florrie were in quarantine, the rash was all over her little body and peeling. Emily knew this was when the disease was at its most infectious. Alice would miss Chas and Florrie dreadfully but had some consolation in that she was back with her mother and had baby Annie to nurture. Her sister Ellen visited every day with Cuthbert and Emily fussed over them all as a devoted grandmother.

Chas nursed Florrie as best he could but she did not improve. She had been in bed for over four weeks, her nose was streaming, she said her ears hurt and she cried when she coughed, clutching her side as she did so. Chas tried several remedies including hearts ease and lovage but nothing seemed to help. In desperation he called Doctor Cooper who after listening to her chest said she had pneumonia and that she must be kept in bed in a warm room and given plenty to drink in the form of cordials and medicinal wines. Her father did his best but Florence Daisy Plant died two days later on the 7th February 1883.

Doctor Cooper visited again to certify the death and take Florrie away. He told Chas to burn all Florrie's clothes and bed linen before allowing baby Annie back home. Chas went to the register office the following day and the burial was arranged for the 12th February at Bonner Hill. Florence was buried in the same plot as her oldest sister Mabel, who she never knew, two babes together. The ceremony was a simple one but with many mourners, Florrie had a loving family in her short life and they were all there, Chas, Alice with baby Annie, Emily, Ellen, Uncle Sam and Aunt Annie. The following week, the Plant family went together to the register office and Mr Harris remembered Chas. Alice registered the birth of Annie May Plant and Mr Harris gave them his heart felt kindest wishes and hoped that a new life could soften their grief at the loss of Florence. Alice, Chas and Annie returned home, it was time to get back to work and put little Annie first.

Alice was very protective of Annie and she thrived. They visited Grannie Gray once a week and her Aunt Ellen was expecting another baby. Annie was the youngest child in Grange Passage and the other children didn't have much to do with her as most of them were now at school. Chas was getting on well with his basketry and the wholesaler was buying everything he could make. He liked working on his own at home with Alice and Annie. They were managing and he did not have to answer to anyone, there was no need to make things more complicated. Alice looked forward to her sister's new baby as a playmate for Annie. Her brothers were all working and Will, now a skilled baker, often gave Alice tips, recipes and ingredients. She enjoyed baking and there was always something sweet in the scullery when visitors called.

Ellen gave birth to baby Elsie the following autumn but there were complications and Ellen did not recover from her confinement. Her husband, Albert, took her down to Wales to convalesce with his mother but she died soon afterwards and he decided to stay down there with his children and remarried. Alice and her mother missed Ellen and Cuthbert very much indeed and Emily was keen to see as much of her new granddaughter Annie as possible.

Meanwhile, Uncle Sam had founded a Ratepayers Association and was now a Town Councillor. He was trying with his friend and colleague Major Macaulay to get the Canbury rubbish dump described in The Surrey Comet as:
> *"a dismal swamp,"*

redeveloped into recreational gardens. His wife was in poor health and Councillor Gray needed a project to occupy his mind. Kingston was enjoying a building boom but many of the ancient buildings had no drainage systems and all the slops flowed directly into the river. A sewage farm had been built to service the new housing estates but the Canbury marshes had been ignored. The sweet sickly smell from the rubbish dump and the sewage farm was particularly strong on hot summer days when the Thames was at its most popular for pleasure seekers. Sam Gray had a vision to make the riverside, downstream from the bridge, a pleasant recreational park for residents and visitors to enjoy the river and its amenities. Uncle Sam would regularly visit Alice, often with petition in hand, to rally the residents and he was always eager to hear her news.

Alice had grieved enough and was pregnant again, this time she had a little boy called Percy Charles George, his big sister was nearly four years old and all was well. When Percy was nearly four they had another girl called Constance Emily and when Connie was nearly three, they had their second son, Sidney James Plant. He was born one month before Annie's tenth birthday; she was a good little helper for her mother when she was not at school. Sid, Annie and Connie had birthdays close together in January and February which brightened up the long dark days. Percy was now six and had just started school. Chas enjoyed all his children with their different personalities. Annie was a real little mother, Percy, adventurous, Connie, a quiet serious child and Sid, a little comedian. They were very crowded in their cottage with only two rooms and they had new tenants upstairs. A Mr & Mrs Charles Thompson, with their adult daughter and son Charles who at twenty-six had been pensioned out of the army reserve. This family constantly complained that the Plant children were noisy and it was time to find somewhere bigger for their large family.

Chapter XVII

Oaklea Passage & Big Changes.

Samuel Gray's wife, Alice's Aunt Annie, died shortly after Percy was born and he fought his grief by pursuing the plan for Canbury with even greater vigour. In 1888 he eventually got agreement after several objections from many councillors who did not want leisure facilities made available to the working people.

Sam built his own house in Gibbon Road and still owned property in Orchard Road and Town End, where he had lived as child with his parents and grandfather. On one of his regular visits to Annies Cottages, Alice and Chas spoke to him about the possibility of them moving away from Grange Passage. Their lease was due for renewal in January and they needed more space. Were any of his houses available to rent and how much would they cost? Uncle Sam owned some of the maltings as well as three tiny Georgian cottages where he grew up in Oaklea Passage. The Town End gravel pits had been filled in and tidied up. Sam had fitted each of his cottages with indoor cold water, gas lighting and its own privy attached to the scullery. The two up, two down, terraced house with a kitchen including range and boiler, along with a small south facing yard was available for rent at £25 a year, but if Chas and Alice wanted it they could have it for £22. This was almost double what they were currently paying and they needed to think about it.

Chas went to the Post Office to check on his savings, he had £26 7s 6d left and he was now regularly earning £1 5s a week. Their biggest expense was coal and food but he thought they should just about be able to manage. The children could walk to the National School in Wood Street. Chas remembered how cold and damp the winters had been when he worked with Mr Benjamin, but it was not much better at Annies Cottages and they would not have difficult neighbours sharing their house. Annie and Connie could have their own bedroom, Percy and Sid the other. Alice and Chas were happy to sleep in the parlour and use the back room as a workshop, but most importantly Alice would have a kitchen and scullery to herself. Alice was very keen to accept Uncle Sam's offer and Chas agreed.

The Plant family moved into their new home at 18 Oaklea Passage in 1896 shortly after Annie's thirteenth birthday. Percy and Connie were sent to their new school in Wood Street and Sid was now three years old. Alice's brother Will, found her a job in a tea shop that had just opened in Thames Street. Jobbins bakery supplied the bread and pastries but they wanted a pudding cook. Alice started work at six every morning and often didn't get home until after six in the evening but the extra seven shillings a week made all the difference to them managing. Annie did not go back to school, she was to stay home and look after the family while Alice went out to work, just as her mother had done. Annie had been a good scholar and missed school but she also liked cooking and enjoyed taking care of Sid and being with her father.

Sometimes Chas, Annie and Sid took a walk along Queens Promenade when Alice was working and the others were at school. Chas was on nodding acquaintance with many of the river men. The ferry near the railway station on Portsmouth Road was owned by Messrs. Budden and Hart. They were experienced boat builders and had set up a thriving business picking up trade from passengers arriving off the trains from London. They had dozens of boats for sale or hire, for the whole season, a day or just an hour. In the summer months the river was crowded with pleasure boaters and on a Sunday the demand to be rowed across to Bushy Park and Hampton Court or Taggs Island was enormous. Chas watched the activity with interest and became very friendly with a wherryman called Bert Mullins, who knew the Gray family.

The following year was Queen Victoria's Diamond Jubilee and Councillor Gray was at the heart of planning the town celebrations along with the Major. An elaborate bandstand had been erected at Canbury Gardens and the extensive lawns, flowerbeds and riverside walks were proving very popular with young and old, rich and poor. On Sunday 23rd June the whole town was festooned with patriotic bunting:

"God Save The Queen"

Banners were hung across the narrow streets in readiness for the following day. The first event was a parade led by the town band marching from the Guildhall to Canbury. All the schools took part, including the National School that Percy and Connie attended. The children were in their Sunday best and waved Union Jacks as they marched along to the delight of the gathered crowd that included Chas, Alice, Annie and Sid. The band took up position in their new bandstand and played all afternoon. It was a hot sultry day and the grounds were set with dozens of trestle tables for the largest picnic event ever to be held in Kingston, before or since.

This was despite the foul air that permeated from what was now called:

"Perfume Parade".

The town's sewage system had been very shoddily built and was almost useless. The Corporation solved the problem by giving planning permission to The Native Guano Company who processed sewage into dried compost

for horticulture. The works were adjacent to Canbury Gardens and the air was permanently filled with the smell of rotting manure, much to the displeasure of Councillor Gray.

Alice and Annie had prepared a magnificent range of pies and puddings. Grannie Gray and George brought cheese, homemade cordials and beer. Minnie was married with a toddler and babe in arms and arrived with Harry and his new wife. Will provided bread and brought his wife and son. Grannie Gray was delighted to have all her children and grandchildren together. Uncle Sam had the next table along with his nephews and nieces from his dear departed wife's family and next to them is brother William came with his wife Charlotte and their eight children. This was the largest family gathering that Chas had ever experienced and he thoroughly enjoyed it.

At dusk the humid heat dispersed into the most beautiful evening and the family walked home tired but cheerful, past the huge bonfire that had been lit on the Fairfield as a beacon to honour Her Majesty's reign of sixty years. The celebrations continued all week, with cycling events along the tow path, the Rowing & Sailing Club Jubilee Regatta, swimming races and the week ended with another bonfire and a spectacular firework display at the Fairfield. This was a week that Chas would never forget.

Sid was now a schoolboy and it was time for his elder brother Percy to leave school and get a job. His school report was not as good as Annie's had been:

"A clever lad, but not attentive in his lessons."

The headmaster recommended placing Percy with Mr Denny the owner of the Victoria Dairy in London Road. He employed several men and provided each of them with a small cart and a pony. The milk churns were delivered by the local farmers after first milking, about four in the morning, to Mr Denny's where the ponies were stabled. His dairymen then tacked up the horses to their carts, each loaded with a churn of eight gallons, over 130 pints of milk, ready to go off on their rounds within the hour. Percy was assigned to Mr Shoesmith, who out of Mr Denny's earshot was called Dick. The round took about four hours and included Gibbon Road, where Percy's Great Uncle Sam lived. Each house left their empty churns by the service door and it was Percy's job to run and collect them, one pint, two pints or five pints brought to Dick to fill to the brim. Percy then walked back, taking care not to spill any and place on the doorstep. At the end of the round they returned to the dairy to load up again for the afternoon delivery. Saturday always took longer when Dick had to collect payment from his customers while Percy minded Jess the pony.

Not long after Percy started work Edward VII became King, after the death of Queen Victoria. The whole country had been in mourning again, but Edward was popular and his coronation in 1902 was welcomed by the people. There was change in the air. Alice was forty-five years old and weary, she was still rising at dawn to work in the tea shop. Chas was making his baskets but had not increased his earnings. Annie was now a skilled cook, taking after her mother with a talent for baking and she enjoyed her domestic duties. Percy was doing well at the dairy, while Connie and Sid were still at school.

Every day Alice found it a little more difficult to get up to go to work, she was breathless and had no energy. The winter of 1903 was extremely damp and Alice was now getting pains in her chest, they came at night and prevented her sleeping. The tea shop was not as busy in the winter, Alice was given notice and came home to her bed in December. Annie was a good nurse and took care of her mother, but by January Alice was unable to get out of bed and was also rather confused. Chas called Doctor Renton who diagnosed a bad heart and bed rest. Chas tried many remedies and sat with Alice in the evenings, but on the 4th February 1904 Alice had a heart attack and died just before Sid's eleventh birthday.

Chas had lost his beloved wife and struggled to cope. Alice had always been very wise in his eyes, he missed her company and struggled to make decisions without her. Annie was twenty-one and tried to reassure her father but he was worried about money and his children. He was determined that none of them would end up in the workhouse. Percy was seventeen and liked by Mr Denny who was very sorry to hear of Mrs Plant's death. The Victoria Dairy had expanded with a new depot in London and Mr Denny had a vacancy on a milk round in Clerkenwell. There was a large house with stables and three of the dairymen lived in. Did Percy want to join them for free lodgings and a pay rise? Percy was delighted and could not wait to tell his father. Chas was pleased for him and relieved, it was time he made his own way in the world and wished him well. They would all miss him and he must keep in touch. Sid was very upset to lose his big brother who often took him down to the river, Chas consoled him and promised to take Sid out on a Sunday to the riverside.

When Percy left, Chas moved upstairs to share Sid's bedroom and the family had a proper parlour for the first time in their lives. Connie was nearly fourteen and ready to leave school. She had been found a domestic placement with an American journalist, Mr George Dussol and his French wife Maria. They leased a house called Frisco, in Woodbines Avenue and required an indoor servant. Connie had learned well from Annie and her mother, she was willing and was expected to cook, clean and organise the laundry. Mr & Madam Dussol wanted a young housemaid they could train because they spent much of their time in London and abroad and needed a servant to look after the house. When they were home Connie's duties were demanding although she rarely had to cook an evening meal as the Dussol's were socialites and ate out a great deal. Connie was given Sunday afternoon off and one Saturday a month, when she always walked home to see her family. Sometimes Annie and Connie met in Kingston when the Dussol's were away. They missed sharing a room together but at least they were living within a short walk from each other. Connie's wages were very low and neither she nor Percy sent money home. Chas now only had to earn enough to feed three mouths but it was still a struggle and he needed to find a way of earning some extra money.

Chapter XVIII

Messrs Budden & Hart, Boat Builders & Watermen.

Chas and Sid went down to the river most Sunday afternoons unless it was pouring with rain. They would always stop and chat to Bert Mullins when he was around and he usually had a bit of a grumble. He hated Sundays, they were the busiest day of the week in the summer and he liked to have the day off with his wife and children. Bert was a Kings Waterman and a staunch member of the A.S.W.L.B, the Amalgamated Society of Watermen, Lightermen and Bargemen. He was a skilled oarsman and worked a single oar wherry most of the time, back and forth across the river or upstream to Hampton and back. He knew everyone who worked on the river, the houseboaters, the members of Kingston Sailing & Rowing Club and the Surbiton Swimming Club who swam from Ravens Eyot in the summer months and the Royal Canoe Club further downstream. Mr Hart, the owner of the boat yard sometimes joined in conversation with Bert and Chas about the complexities of running a ferry on such a busy stretch of water and Bert would always interject with a complaint about something.

Mr Budden and Mr Hart were relative newcomers to Thameside at Town End and their boathouse was the closest ferry crossing to the mainline railway. Their premises were luxurious; they had over forty pleasure boats of all sizes and kinds including rowing boats, punts, outriggers, canoes, and wherries for hire and for sale. There were several boatyards along the Kingston stretch, Turks at Albany Park by Canbury Gardens and the famous Taggs Island with its luxury hotel and boatyards in Molesey and Kingston. There were rumours printed in The Surrey Comet that George Tagg was suffering financial problems and his Thames Hotel was losing popularity.

> *"The Thames Hotel had been a Mecca for society; Royalty, nobility and millionaires rubbed shoulders with theatrical, artistic and literary folk, swells, squanderers and shadowy gents of all kinds. During the season its well-kept lawn, dotted with chairs and tables, presented a very gay scene, thronged with well known people, especially at the week-ends when celebrities could be seen in great numbers."*

Mr Hart believed that he and Mr Budden could fill part of the gap that George Tagg was leaving and cater for the needs of rowing men with their boatbuilding and repair shop, also hiring out and selling boats alongside the running of the ferry.

Chas and Sid both enjoyed watching the boats come and go with the rich people promenading and mucking about on the river. They had no idea who these people were but their antics were fun to watch. Sometimes when the river was quiet Bert would take them out in his one-man wherry and let Chas take the oars, he was a naturally strong sculler and he had a good feel for the movement of the boat and the tide. Bert knew that Chas was looking to earn some extra money and suggested that he could do some casual work on a Sunday to give Bert a day off. Chas needed a bit of training and he would have to join the A.S.W.L.B. but the tips were good and it was all cash in hand. Chas thought it was an excellent idea and they both went to see Mr Hart who was open to the proposal but must talk to Mr Budden first.

Bert and Chas arranged to meet up the following Tuesday morning for some sculling practise in a two-man wherry. It was pouring with rain but they went out anyway. Chas struggled to keep up with Bert but his technique improved just in that one session. They disembarked and went into Mr Hart's office to discover that Mr Budden had agreed in principal but the company could not pay Chas due to insurance restrictions. If he was on the payroll and there was an accident the company would be responsible. Chas had to take on the work at his own risk and he would be liable if the boat suffered any damage. Bert did not think this was a problem and pointed out that on a good day Chas could get three or four gold sovereigns in tips, Chas readily agreed. Throughout April, each Sunday, Chas and Sid walked down to the boatyard and Bert used the two-man wherry for any patrons wanting to cross the river, with Chas as his assistant oarsman. Any tips received were shared equally. Sid watched from the riverbank and amused himself with skimming stones or playing marbles with the riverboat boys who were also his school chums. Sometimes Mr Hart would give him a cleaning job to do and pay him three pence.

Mrs Mullins had asked Bert if he could take the day off on May Day, she and the children were going to the fair and the little ones had been chosen by Sunday School to dance around the maypole. Bert thought Chas was good enough to man his own wherry now and Mr Hart was in agreement. May Day dawned to a bitter easterly wind and Chas made his way down to the boatyard for nine-o-clock. Unusually, Connie had stayed over the night before with Annie, her employers were in France and her monthly Saturday off had coincided with the May Day holiday. Annie, Connie and Sid were all off to the fair, wrapped up well in their winter clothes and hoped their father would get on well with the ferry.

Chas had been issued a blue wherryman's blazer and peaked cap. He was wearing his Macintosh leggings. The river was busy as usual with rowers, sailing boats and pleasure steamers but there were not many patrons getting off the train. At last about eleven his first passengers boarded, two elderly gentlemen wanting to cross the river to Bushy Park. The wind was very strong, Chas mustered all his strength to row into the wind and delivered his cargo without incident, the gentlemen disembarked, tipped him with a half crown and departed. Chas then rowed back in a following wind feeling very pleased with himself. The afternoon brought more customers and on one occasion he was able to return with passengers on board. Every crossing resulted in a tip varying from six pence, to one gold sovereign. His first day had not been busy, nothing had gone wrong and he was £1 15s 6d better off, more than he earned in a whole week from his basketry.

He arrived home just after dark very cold and hungry, his children were still at the fair. Annie had left out a pig trotter and some bread pudding for his supper, he heated some port wine on the range to warm himself up and settled down to his meal. Annie and Sid arrived home shortly afterwards, Sid was clutching a coconut, it had been a happy day. Chas meanwhile had laid out his tips on the table and Annie could not believe her eyes. The following day Chas went to see Bert and told him the news. Bert was pleased for him but a bit under the weather, the beer at the May Fair was free flowing and Bert had got rather carried away. It was arranged that Chas would cover Bert in two weeks' time on the 14th May. Sam Gray soon heard about the new wherryman and came to see Chas at Oaklea Passage. He had been worried that Chas may not be able to manage and was pleased that the family could afford to stay on at the house for the foreseeable future.

The spring and summer was busy for Chas, he rarely had a day off. Most Sundays Sid would go with him to the boatyard, at least for half a day and Annie amused herself at home. Bert liked working on the regatta and race days because it gave him a close-up view of the events and prime position to cheer on his friends and the competitors. However, he was pleased not to work on hot sultry Sundays when crowds of train passengers invaded the town, all wanting to cross the river at the same time. Chas was already very competent and had a polite charm that encouraged his patrons to tip him well. On busy days he could pick up passengers in both directions and one particular Sunday in August he came home with five gold sovereigns, three half sovereigns, one silver crown and three half-crowns amounting to £7 2s 6d, nearly two months earnings as a basketmaker.

The theatrical folk were the best tippers and he thoroughly enjoyed studying their extraordinary behaviour. He did not envy the rich people, he thought them rather amusing, but there was one particular gentleman who made an impression. He and his intended wife, Miss Drury-Lowe, were attending a reception for "The Society of the Linked Ring" at The Thames Hotel on Taggs Island one busy Sunday afternoon and Chas rowed them across the river. Mr Walter Colls, who described himself as an aquafortist, was very interested in the way the sunlight fell on the water as the wherry crossed the current. He asked Chas many questions about the tides and the weather. The gentleman tipped Chas handsomely with a gold sovereign and asked if he could return for them about six-o-clock.

Chas was delighted and made sure he was ready and waiting in good time. Mr Colls was a distinguished looking man with strong eyebrows, a finely trimmed beard and moustache. There was something about his eyes that reminded Chas of his daughters Annie and Connie. The gentleman talked to Chas all the way back, a mist was rising off the water and he praised Chas's rowing skills through the busy river traffic. When they alighted at Budden & Hart he thanked Chas, shook his hand, gave him another gold sovereign and a very stylish visiting card. Chas doffed his cap in appreciation.

> COPPERPLATE PHOTO. ETCHING AND ENGRAVING
> **MR WALTER L. COLLS**
>
> PHOTOGRAPHS FROM NATURE, PICTURES, ENGRAVINGS, DRAWINGS
> NUMEROUS MEDALS HAVE BEEN AWARDED & PRESS NOTICES FOR EXCELLENCE OF WORK
>
> ESTIMATES MAY BE OBTAINED ON APPLICATION AT THE STUDIOS PERSONALLY OR BY LETTER
> **CASTELNAU GARDENS, BARNES, SURREY.**

Chas moored up the wherry and went into Mr Hart's office, did he know who the gentleman was that he had just brought back? Mr Hart did not, but when Chas showed him the visiting card, he remembered something he had read in The Surrey Comet. The reception had been held in Mr Colls honour by a photographic society. He was a leading light in the production of photogravures and was the son of a Bond Street art dealer, called Mr Lebbeus Colls. This meant nothing to Chas but he took the card home and put it in his savings tin for safe keeping. Chas did not remember his mother Mercy and never knew her maiden name. He had forgotten all the family stories that his sister told him when he was tiny about the millers, corn merchants and artists that lived in Norfolk and London. Chas recognised a family resemblance in Mr Colls, because they were first cousins and shared the same grandparents, Richard and Sarah Hood Colls. They did not meet again and neither knew they were related. That was the last time Chas had contact with any of his relations. He never heard again from Fred or his sisters and they were all unaware of their connection to the influential Colls family.

The river quietened down in October and Chas, although still working most Sundays was only taking a few coppers in tips. He made sure he was always available for work if Bert or any of the other wherryman wanted the day off because he did not want to lose his summer income. The Surrey Comet reported that George Tagg was bankrupt and there was to be an auction of all his assets in December. Mr Budden and Mr Hart were interested in some of the boats and the auction drew a large crowd, including Chas, Bert and Sam Gray. The place was heaving with boating and river men, many of whom had worked for the Tagg family. The auction did not go well and many lots were withdrawn for not reaching their reserve. Chas was pleased to see Mr Budden win a steam launch and a job lot of punts and canoes. Sam Gray bought some flags and bunting for future municipal events. Many lots remained unsold and the heyday of Taggs Thames Hotel was over. This would affect the ferry in the months to come but for the time being Chas was still enjoying his casual work as a wherryman.

The Red Lion on the corner of Red Lion Lane and Ewell Road, Tolworth.

Chapter XIX

The Tolworth Tram & Lenelby Road.

The following two boating seasons that ran from March to October were very good for Chas. He worked every Sunday and on May Day his tips were numerous gold sovereigns, he was equal to the other wherrymen. Annie took on a cleaning job in The Griffin Hotel, it was a busy place with a valet, two chambermaids and two parlour maids in addition to the cooks and barmaids. Annie went in for a few hours each day to pick up any extra work that needed doing for a few shillings. Connie was very settled at the Dussol household and Percy had written to say he had met a young lady called Mabel Giles, a florist and daughter of a solicitor's clerk. Chas was pleased for Percy and now there was just Sid, who would very soon be leaving school. He did worry that both Annie and Connie worked too hard and hoped they would meet someone to marry and have children of their own, as Chas had done nearly thirty years earlier.

There was a great deal of bad news in the papers, the suffragettes were causing a lot of trouble in London and there had been some grisly murders in Richmond and Camden Town. Chas knew the gypsies on Taggs Island and was very upset when he heard they had been evicted by the new owner. He often talked to them while waiting for his fare back across the river and he respected their way of life. They made a poor living from hedgerow basketry and Chas was always interested in what they made. Some of them were related to the Wells family and it made him wonder about Dan and Albert who moved away after Mr Benjamin died.

There was some good news, The London United Tramway Company had built, with the support of Surbiton and Kingston Corporation, an electric service from Kingston via Surbiton to Tolworth. There had been huge disruption throughout 1905 with the building of the tracks but in 1906 on the 1st March the first trams were operational. Chas thought it would be a nice treat on his birthday to take Annie, Connie and Sid on the tram to Tolworth. They walked to the station and boarded the open topped double decker and climbed the stairs to get the best view on their journey. The smart conductor in his black uniform and peaked cap regaled with the letters L.U.T. and a ticket machine around his neck was shouting:

> *"Fares please. Fares please. How much to Tolworth?*
> *1/- single or 1/8d return."*

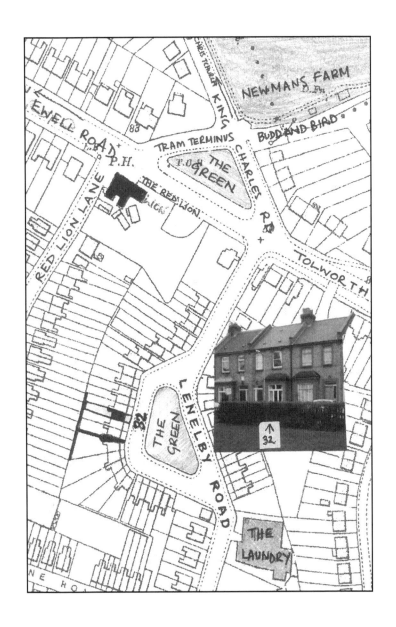

Chas bought four, 1/- tickets and before they knew it they had arrived at The Red Lion, in just twenty minutes. The view from the top of the tram was amazing, they could see into the gardens of the big houses and everything looked so grand. On arrival at Crescent Gardens opposite The Red Lion they all jumped off and walked along Red Lion Lane where Henry Gray had grown up and worked. They walked past the new sewage works where Uncle Harry lived and worked and then back to Ewell Road.

Chas wanted to look at the new houses being built in Lenelby Road. There was a triangular green with pretty terraced villa cottages arranged all around. In the corner was a laundry with a farm across the road. There was no dampness in the air and more importantly no strong smell of rotting manure or maltings. The houses were advertised to include internal mains cold tap, solid fuel range and electric light with individual water closet and private yard. Chas thought this would be a very nice place to live. They all walked back home up the hill to Town End and Chas was very eager to find out how much it would cost to live in Tolworth. The lease for number 32 was £18 a year, or a five year' lease reduced from £90 to £80. Chas checked his savings and after his additions from tips he had enough to pay £20 and the rest in weekly instalments, with interest over three years. Chas knew that Sam Gray, now 72 wanted to sell his houses in Oaklea Passage and buy shares in the Kingston Gas Company. His orphaned nephew, Will Miles, who lived with him, was a clerk at the Gas Company and Sam wanted to make sure he and his sister were well looked after.

The move to Tolworth was embraced by them all, except Connie, who thought it was too far away. Sid was delighted to be taken out of school and ready to do whatever his father suggested. Annie had a stoic nature and was happy to go along with the idea, the move to 32 Lenelby Road went ahead in January 1908 when Sid was 14. Chas paid for a five year' lease on his new Edwardian house that had a fireplace and one electric light in every room with one electric plug in the parlour and the kitchen. Annie had her own bedroom to be shared with Connie, when she visited. Chas and Sid the other. Chas intended to make his baskets in the front parlour and the kitchen with its solid fuel range was where they would all live, eat and also bathe once a week in a tin bath after the copper had been boiled up on laundry day. The west facing yard was long and thin and sufficient to grow a few herbs and vegetables with space for a couple of sheds to store willow and other miscellaneous items.

Chas intended to continue with the wherrying, at least through the summer months. The walk up to Surbiton took one half hour and Bert was still keen to take Sunday off. Moving day was helped greatly by one of Bert's bargee acquaintances Jack Stubbins, who arrived at Oaklea Passage on his horse and cart. Molly the shire horse was a gentle steady creature used to pulling the barge and stood patiently while her master Jack, along with Chas and Sid loaded up the cart. Annie was run ragged packing up the breakables in baskets, all the pots and pans went in the tin bath and their clothes were tied up in the bedlinen. Four iron bedsteads were arranged around the edge of the cart to hold everything in. The table was upside down with chairs on top and then the mattresses, all loaded and covered with a tarpaulin in case of rain. There was room up front for Annie to ride with Jack. Molly walked at a very leisurely pace down Surbiton Hill to Tolworth with Chas and Sid walking behind. When they arrived at number 32 their new landlord was waiting with papers to sign and the keys. Chas felt pleased with himself, he was now totally independent. The unloading did not take long and Jack departed with Molly after a welcome jug of beer at The Red Lion and a gold sovereign for his trouble.

The family settled in quickly to their new home, Chas got back to work immediately and took Sid over the road to Newmans Farm who were advertising for agricultural labourers. Annie found some early morning cleaning work at a shop on the Ewell Road and Connie visited once a month on her day off. She always walked down to Tolworth but sometimes caught the tram back if the weather was bad, she could not really afford the one shilling fare and Chas usually gave it to her.

It proved difficult for Chas to get his baskets to his regular wholesaler in Kingston, it was a long walk and he needed a cart. As usual Bert knew someone, a coal merchant who was selling one of his hand carts, it was perfect for Chas but in bad repair. Chas occupied himself the following week, by fixing the broken planks, cleaning, painting and stabilising the loose wheels. The finished article in dark green looked very fine when it was loaded with baskets and Chas discovered that he could sell them directly as he walked through the streets from Tolworth to Kingston. He painted a sign:

Wet Washing Baskets
7/6d & 9/6d

Sometimes he sold one or two on the way to the wholesaler who gave him two shillings less and sold them on for double the price. He always made sure the sign was hidden when he arrived at the mill, the wholesaler did not take kindly to competition. Several of Chas's neighbours also bought his handiwork and the Tolworth Laundry were constantly asking him to repair their own industrial baskets. Chas was very busy indeed and also started making baby cribs like the one he had made for Mabel and used for all his children.

Chas still enjoyed working on the river, he liked the camaraderie and watching the people, but the walk on a cold wet Sunday morning when he knew there would not be much trade started to wear him down. After two more seasons he decided to stop. Bert asked if he would still cover sometimes on high days and holidays, Chas agreed, the occasional tip would be very welcome. Connie also came back home because her employers were moving to France and she did not want to work for the incoming family. The Dussols gave Connie a good reference and she managed to find a placement in a big house on Surbiton Hill. Sid was doing well at the farm, he liked working with the animals and had become a competent cowman. Chas expected all of them to pay for their keep, but there was still not quite enough each week to make ends meet. Chas only had a few pounds left in his savings and was keen to keep that for emergencies.

The solution was to get a lodger, an extra ten shillings a week would make all the difference. Chas could move down to the front parlour and the lodger share with Sid. The task was delegated to Sid who knew immediately who to ask. His friend Frank was unhappy in his lodgings with his half-brother Arthur at number 8. The Sherwood boys worked at Newmans Farm with Sid, they were much older than Frank and were hard, tough drinking men who did heavy labour out in the fields. Frank had been living with his recently widowed mother Martha and was a quiet gentle soul, he did not like lodging with Arthur who was a bully to his wife and children. The house was crowded and Frank shared with Percy, Arthur's only son, he would much prefer to share a room with his friend Sid.

Frank was four years older than Sid but Chas warmed to him immediately, he had a deprived childhood and Chas recognised a sadness in him. Frank's father was a brawling drunkard who rejected Frank at birth and favoured his older sons. His mother was kind and gentle but suffered terribly at the hands of her husband. They lived in Red Lion Lane and she had eight children by him plus two stepsons from his previous marriage to her elder sister, Maria. Frank was not sent to school and could not read or write. His mother would put Frank and his little brother Charles to sleep at night in the loft over the cow shed, to avoid any confrontation when their father and his boys came home after a hard night's drinking. Frank was kind like his mother and fitted in very well at the Plant household. He got on famously with Sid, Connie and especially Annie. Chas was very pleased with his new lodger.

Frank did not work on the farm, he was a building's labourer and when he moved in with the Plants he was working in Leatherhead as a bricklayer's scaffolder. He left Tolworth at 4.30 every Monday morning and did not return until late Saturday, tired after his hard week and long walk home. He dossed down in cheap lodgings during the week with the navvies and hated their drunkenness. It cost him sixpence a night and he was pleased to return to Tolworth for a good night's rest before having to do it all again the following week. This job lasted a few months and Chas felt bad about taking ten shillings off Frank and reduced it to five shillings while he was away. Frank's scaffolding hammer was his guarantee of work. It was double headed, a hammer one side and a spurred notched axe on the other. The spur was most important and used to tension the tying of the standards (uprights) at the marrying of ledgers (verticals) with cord, hemp or galvanised iron wire. The standards and ledgers were made of cane, wood or iron, depending on the purpose of the scaffold and the tying was vital to the safety of the workers. The work was hard and dangerous but not dissimilar to basketry and Frank was always interested in what Chas was making.

Frank's next job was more local, working on the railway at Chessington and it gave the family a chance to get to know each other better. Annie had been good at reading and writing at school and Frank asked her if she would teach him to read. She was a patient teacher and there was always a lot of laughing in the process. Annie loved people like her father and it was nice to have the house filled with laughter again as it was when Alice was alive and the children were young. Sid was always up for a joke and reminded Chas of himself when he was at school with Abe, he wondered if Abe was married with children. Connie enjoyed music and had been given a phonograph by her mistress, Mrs Myer, whose husband had purchased a new gramophone with disc records. Many people had a piano but Chas had no space or money for such a luxury. The phonograph proved to be a great success, particularly when they could sing along to the popular songs of the day.

Annie and Frank were getting on famously, Annie had never been so happy. She was older than Frank and her motherly nature warmed to his kind and gentle ways. He was an attractive man with a strong jaw and sparkling eyes. Frank thought Annie very pretty with her large doleful eyes, dainty nose and sweet mouth. Neither were experienced in romantic matters but romance did blossom on Frank's birthday in 1912 and six months later Annie thought she could be with child. She worried about telling Frank and her father but Chas had noticed a change in Annie and was not surprised when she told him that she was having Frank's baby. Frank was delighted and agreed to marry Annie immediately.

On 21st June 1913 Frank and Annie took the tram to Kingston and were married in the presence of strangers at the register office. There were no photographs, but they did come straight home and have a little party in the house with Chas, Connie and Sid. A few weeks later Annie gave birth, after a bit of trouble and help from the midwife to Charles Frank Sherwood, a strong healthy boy with a mass of black hair. Chas could not have been more pleased, he had his first grandchild, a boy, named after him and life was perfect. He had no idea that his eldest son Percy was also married with two daughters.

Chapter XX

The Great War.

Baby Charlie got a lot of attention from his mother and Auntie Connie who all now shared a bedroom. Annie left home at a quarter past five each morning for her part time cleaning job and Connie gave the baby his breakfast before also going to work. Frank often had a half hour walk to his site and usually left just before sunrise. Sid always rushed out of the door at dawn to the farm just across the road. Chas was left in charge of the baby until Annie returned at about nine, ready for the day's chores and he relished that time with his grandson. When he was tiny, the baby was left upstairs to sleep and play while Annie was working, but as he grew and started taking notice of things Chas would settle him in a corner of the parlour while he worked on his baskets and told him stories. This time reminded him of his own children when they were little, particularly little Florrie, bless her.

The following spring, Charlie was crawling and Frank built a playpen in the yard. Chas sat outside and worked on his baskets while Charlie chattered and played next to him throughout the summer. Frank was a country boy and suggested they get some rabbits to raise for meat, he built a hutch and the toddler loved watching and stroking the rabbits and feeding them greens. The newspapers made very gloomy headlines, every week there was another crisis in The Balkans and now France was joining in the war against Austria and Germany. On 4th August 1914, five days before baby Charlie's first birthday Great Britain declared war on Germany.

"Your King and Country Need You to Enlist Now"

Lord Kitchener, an experienced soldier from the Boer War and the new "Secretary of State of War" appointed by Mr Asquith, the Prime Minister, was constantly reported in the newspapers. He was a distinguished looking man with strong features and a large Victorian moustache, his face appeared everywhere encouraging young men to join up to fight for their country. Chas was worried for his boys, he had heard many stories from old soldiers when working on the river and he did not want any of his family to suffer the horror and bloodshed that war could bring. Sid was quite keen to join up but Frank and Chas talked him out of it. Bill Sherwood, one of Frank's older brothers joined the regular army when Frank was a baby to escape his father's abuse and on his rare visits home, his stories about army life frightened Frank. This was enough for the time being to put Sid off.

Chas decided to write to Percy at The Victoria Dairy to find out his intentions. Percy had not told his father that he had moved, but he was still working at the dairy. He felt a bit guilty about not keeping in touch and showed the letter to his wife Mabel who offered to write back on his behalf.

31 Elfort Road,
Highbury,
London.

Dear Father,

I hope I find you well. I am sorry I have not written before but am pleased to tell you I am now married to Mabel and we have two daughters, Margaret is five years and Kathleen nearly three. I shall not be volunteering into the army. My duty is to my wife and children. Please give my kind wishes to my sisters and Sid.

Yours truly,   Percy.

Chas was glad that Percy was settled with a family. He was very pleased to hear that he had two granddaughters and hoped he would meet them one day. He showed the letter to his children and then placed it in his savings tin, as a keepsake.

The Great War, as it was now being called, affected everyone, rich and poor. Thousands of men had volunteered and left their families behind only to be killed on the frontline. The newspapers talked of the success and victories of the British Army over the "Terrible Hunn" in Europe and gave vivid descriptions of awful atrocities carried out by the enemy. The Germans started sending Zeppelins over to bomb British towns and London suffered the most. The sight of a large sausage shaped balloon floating in the sky, put the fear of God into people and the deafening sound of anti-aircraft guns on the ground echoed for miles around. The War Office released carefully worded propaganda to the newspapers to exaggerate reports of destruction and tragedy in the name of patriotism and to encourage more volunteers. Sid was ready to join up and Chas could not find a reason to argue against it, they were all frightened for their families and the Germans had to be stopped.

In June 1915 Sidney James Plant aged 22 went to the recruiting office in Kingston and signed up with the East Surrey Regiment, he was immediately billeted to 12th Battalion. The following month, with almost no training, he was sent to France to support the troops already at the Somme. It was an adventure and Sid made some good friends but the experience was too traumatic for him to discuss when he came home on leave. On his return he was posted to 1st Battalion taking him back again to the Western Front and the following year again in the 12th for the final push. He miraculously survived the whole war and was demobbed in early 1919. He came back home to Tolworth not quite the same happy go lucky chap that had left four years earlier. He never talked about his experiences at the Somme in mixed company.

Chas saw that Sid on his first leave when they still shared a room, had suffered greatly. He had terrifying nightmares and only told his father snippets of what it was like in the trenches. Frank now felt that he should do his bit, it was rumoured that conscription was being brought in for single men between the age of eighteen and thirty. Frank was 27 and married with a child but his brother Bill had just been killed in action and he decided to volunteer before he was conscripted.

Connie had told Annie about her employer's latest hobby of photography and shown her a picture that Mr Myers had developed in his own darkroom of Connie at work in Mr and Mrs Myers kitchen. Annie thought it would be a nice idea to have all their photographs taken as a keepsake for Frank. Connie asked Mrs Myers if her husband would be willing to take another photograph of her, with her sister and nephew. Mr Myers was delighted to oblige and suggested the following Sunday after church. The Plants were not regular churchgoers but occasionally attended a service at Saint Matthew's on the corner of Ravenswood Avenue, where the Myers lived.

Charlie was now three with beautiful blonde curls and Annie dressed him up in his Sunday best, a white sailor suit with a large navy blue taffeta bow. He looked just like Bubbles in the Pears Soap advert. Annie and Connie both wore white muslin blouses and made sure their hair was tied back in a fashionable bun. The picture was taken at Saint Matthew's Church outside the vestry door, with Annie to the right, on a bright Sunday afternoon in June. Mr Myers was very pleased with the results after he returned home and developed several copies from his glass negative. Connie and Chas were extremely grateful to Mr Myers who was very humble in accepting praise, he was after all said and done just an amateur.

The tiny sepia photograph was admired by them all. Chas put his in the savings tin, Annie stood hers in a brass frame on the parlour cupboard and Frank placed his in his breast pocket next to his heart. It was time for Frank to leave; Annie kissed him and gave him a cake, Chas, two sovereigns and baby Charlie a big hug. Frank knew he must do his duty and hid the fact that he was very scared.

Frank Sherwood joined the 13th Battalion of the East Surrey Regiment in June 1916 and his unit went straight to the Western Front with no training. Frank half thought he might meet up with Sid among the thousands of men already there. The allies had progressed forward and it was not long before it was Frank's turn to go over the top and leave the relative safety of the trenches. Frank ran with his gun aimed at the enemy firing line and immediately fell to the ground, he had been shot in the leg. Many of his unit had also gone down, some were screaming and groaning, others were already dead. Frank lay there quietly until the gunshot died down, his unit had retreated and now the Germans were checking the battlefield for survivors. A young German soldier found him and made him stand, pointed to his leg and shouted:

"Gehen, Gehen"

he wanted Frank to walk with the other walking wounded, German and British, they all helped each other back to the German camp at the French town of Saint Quentin.

There were no inhabitants left in the town, only German soldiers and their prisoners. The buildings had been wrecked and ransacked. Frank and his comrades were led to a large empty factory building where they were checked for injuries and given a billy can of cold water. Frank's injury was a large flesh wound. He was handed a bandage, told to dress it himself and sent off to another building with the other men who were fit to work. The following day they were given their first daily ration, one hard biscuit with hot water in their tin cup to soften it and make it edible. The Germans were making the P.O.W.'s build concrete dug outs along what later became known as the Hindenburg Line. They were preparing for an organised retreat because the allies were breaking their ranks. The Germans were aggressive and Frank was terrified.

He was used to hard labour and coped well with the work that required digging and the mixing of concrete. The fighting could be heard as a constant distant rumble and all the prisoners lived in the hope that the allies would break through the enemy line very soon and release them. The overhead bombing raids were very frightening and the lack of food was now starting to affect them all. The prisoners were tired, hungry and cold. They had all their possessions stripped from them and were not allowed to keep diaries or even have writing paper. Frank treasured his photograph of Annie and Charlie and kept it close to his heart away from prying eyes. Each prisoner was given permission to write one letter a month, but the paper had to be purchased from the commandant. Frank wanted to write and tell Annie he was alive and he asked a fellow prisoner to help him, after buying the paper and a pen with one of his gold sovereigns.

Annie had received a letter from Frank's regiment telling her he was lost in action, she thought he was dead. When Frank's letter arrived in November 1916 she did not want to open it. Annie, Chas and little Charlie all sat round the table while she read:

Dearest Annie.
I am writing to tell you I am alive and a prisoner of the German's in France. They make us work hard but I am alright and think of you all at home. I hope your father is keeping well and looking after you and little Charlie while I am away.
Your ever-loving husband,   Frank.

Annie and Chas were both crying with tears of joy, little Charlie didn't understand but knew it was about Daddy.

The winter on the Somme was severe, with mist, snow and heavy rain that made the air thick and the mud toxic. There was not much news from England, a few prisoners received parcels from home but the hungry German soldiers often stole the contents. Red Cross parcels containing biscuits, cigarettes and tobacco were also raided and rarely reached the prisoners. At last the winter was coming to an end, it was March and soon the sunshine would warm the fields and dry out the mud. The rumble from the fighting seemed to be getting closer and the German officers were becoming more hostile towards the P.O.W.'s. On 17th March 1917 the allies broke through to Saint Quentin only to be faced with an organised German frontline that was ready to fight back. The air raids increased and the guns were very close.

Frank thought the war would soon end and kept that hope for another year, through a fiercely cold winter with continual rain, sleet and snow. He and his fellow inmates were resigned to their drudgery, many had died and most were ill from starvation and hypothermia. Frank was emaciated, but his leg had healed and he was strong enough to work, he was one of the lucky ones. Just when he thought life was never going to change activity in the sky increased, the allies were sending reconnaissance aircraft and the Germans had low morale and were jumpy. On the 8th October 1918 news came from the camp commandant that there was an armistice and fighting should cease. The Germans immediately left the camp, deserting hundreds of bewildered prisoners who were free to wander about the town ruins. Frank joined those who could walk, they crossed the Hindenburg Line and kept walking westward for hours until they met the allied troops. It was a happy but reserved reunion, hundreds of emaciated P.O.W.'s in rags, shook the hands of exhausted Tommies, they were all in shock. Repatriation for the prisoners was very fast. They were transported to Calais by The Red Cross and Frank was already back in England at Woolwich when the war was declared over on the 11th November 1918.

During the three years that Frank was away, Charlie had grown into a little boy and it was almost time for him to start school. He did not know who Frank was when he returned, he thought Chas was his father. Chas had been a good grandfather and Charlie loved sitting with him and hearing his stories. Frank was so very thin when he came home that Annie wept and made it her duty to nurse him back to health. He struggled to eat much to start with, meat and fish were too rich and made him sick but Annie persevered, despite meat, butter and margarine being rationed. Frank brought back a hard biscuit from France to show them his daily ration. Annie was shocked and set about making nice biscuits, fruit loaves and cakes, with the best butter, just for Frank. Her rock cakes were always the butt of jokes in the house because they were sweet, short and delicious unlike Frank's biscuit that was hard and unpalatable. This increase in cooking activity pleased the rest of the family, who all enjoyed Annie's baking, they were a proper family again.

Frank needed to rest, build his strength and get to know his son. It took a few months for him to return to his old cheerful ways but little Charlie and his Annie helped immensely. Chas was so pleased that Frank was safely home and could see that his beloved daughter was happy to have her husband back. Little Charlie was a lively lad and had kept them all amused while Frank was away and now he would also contribute to bringing Frank back to good health.

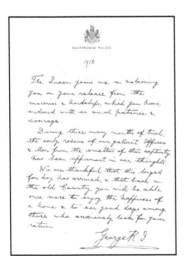

Shortly before Christmas, a letter arrived for Frank, from the King. George V.
Annie read it to him.

"The Queen joins me in welcoming you on your release from the miseries and hardships which you have endured with so much patience and courage.

During these many months of trial, the early rescue of our gallant Officers and Men from the cruelties of their captivity have been uppermost in our thoughts."

We are thankful that this longed for day has arrived and that back in the old country you will be able ...."

Frank angrily snatched the letter away from Annie and threw it on the floor shouting:

> *"The war is done with, I want none of it."*

Annie picked it up later and showed it to Chas who put it in his savings tin.

Chas was worried about Sid who had not yet returned and in January Chas received another letter from Percy's wife Mabel. Percy had also volunteered and joined The Royal Horse and Field Artillery in December 1915. Chas's third granddaughter was born exactly nine months later on 12th September 1916. Percy did not see action immediately but was sent with the Expeditionary Force to the Somme in 1917. Mabel also wrote to Percy's Regiment to ask if they had news of her husband. She knew he was at Saint Quentin in March 1918 and that his division had seen action because it had been reported in the newspapers. This upset Chas and Frank as they both realised that Percy could be one of those killed in the build-up to Frank's release. In February news came that Percy had arrived home to his wife and daughters, a little confused (now known as shell shock) but otherwise in good health. A few days later Sid walked through the door, Chas could relax, both his sons were home safely and his family was complete.

While the men were away fighting, life carried on much the same at home. Chas made his baskets and Connie went to work in Ravenswood Avenue. Chas and Charlie spent a lot of time together while Annie busied herself with household chores. She loved people and liked a bit of fun like her father, she and her sister often sat in the evenings and listened to Chas telling stories about his customers on the ferry and the antics of the river folk, always exaggerated greatly for dramatic effect. With the men away at war Newmans Farm needed labourers and Annie helped out with the strawberry and the potato harvest. Many women were working full time on the land but Annie preferred her cleaning job. She took Charlie potato picking, it was hard work, the plough lifted the tubers and the pickers followed behind finding the spuds and loading them into baskets. Charlie loved finding them and getting very muddy:

> *"Here is another and another one."*

Chas was sixty-five years old and suffering from lumbago and arthritis in his back and hands, just like Mr Benjamin. He mixed up an aconite potion to ease the pain and made a wooden bench to work at from the comfort of a wooden stall. He no longer walked to the wholesaler in Mill Street, he relied on word of mouth and just sold his baskets to friends and neighbours.

Frank and Sid had a great deal to talk about when they shared their room and Chas listened quietly. They told each other things that were never discussed beyond those walls, Annie did not know the half of it. Chas was a good listener, Sid and Frank felt they could speak freely in front of him and that helped both of them in their recovery.

Chapter XXI

Charlie Plant's Greatest Achievement.

Following the return of all his boys the year proved to be an eventful one. Chas worried that Sid had lost his youth and Frank had missed his son Charlie growing up but they were all very lucky compared to many families who had lost their sons, husbands and fathers. Sid was in a rush to get on with life and started courting Millie Dopson from Tolworth Laundry. She was a sweet girl and much younger than Sid but she fitted in with the Plant household very easily and it was obvious to Chas that Sid was in love.

Connie started walking out with Percy Sherwood, the son of Frank's half-brother Arthur, they all still lived at 8 Lenelby Road where Frank had lodged previously. Arthur's son Percy was also in a rush, he had just been released from the army and wanted to get away from his father who ruled with a rod of iron over him and his five sisters. He was two years younger than Connie and swept her off her feet, Chas liked him but Frank was suspicious and spoke to Annie about his concerns. Annie, who always thought the best of people, said there was no need to worry, she knew Connie was happy. In August Connie married Percy at Kingston register office with Percy's father Arthur and his sister May as witnesses. They caught the tram back to The Red Lion where the Sherwoods and the Plants all joined them for a celebratory drink in the pub. Frank and Annie were the first to leave with little Charlie, and Chas joined them, he struggled with his walking stick and welcomed a helping hand from Annie. Connie stayed with Percy from then on and shortly afterwards moved to Wimbledon where Percy worked as a railway porter. Connie got a job as an assistant in a wet fish shop and she was missed dreadfully by Annie and Chas.

The following Christmas was due to be a happy one. Frank had put on weight and Sid was back to his cheeky self. He had asked Millie to marry him and the wedding was booked at the register office for Saturday 3rd January. Chas had received a card from Percy with a photograph of his three granddaughters and Connie planned to visit Christmas Day while her husband saw his family across the road. Annie started the preparations in October with the making of mincemeat, plum pudding and a fruit cake that was spiked with brandy each week before being iced. The cake was to be saved for Sid and Millie's wedding. Sid had part share in a pig they were rearing at the farm and one quarter was promised for Christmas including a whole leg. Chas tended his brassicas and Frank took Charlie scrumping, a basket load of Bramleys had been made into preserves and some delicious apple pies.

Christmas arrived and was great fun. Connie did not stay long, she was expected to eat with the Sherwoods. Millie helped Annie with the cooking, while Frank prepared all the vegetables. Chas and Sid played cards with Charlie in the parlour and they all had a delicious feast and a lovely day. There was plenty of food left over for the wedding the following week. Chas reminisced to Sid about Alice, they had married exactly 43 years earlier in 1877. Sid was only 10 when Alice died, he remembered his mother and liked listening to his father's stories about her. Sid had asked Frank to be his best man and Annie was to be a witness. Millie's family lived in Churt and were not able to come to the wedding. The four of them set off for the register office on the tram while Chas stayed at home with Charlie and told him all about his own wedding and his first day out to The Derby with his beloved Alice. After the ceremony the newlyweds came straight back to the house where Annie had laid out a table of cold meats and preserves and the wedding cake. There was a lot of laughing and singing and even a bit of dancing just like Chas's wedding all those years earlier.

Millie moved in with Sid and the sleeping arrangements were changed round again. Frank now shared Annie's room with Charlie so that Sid and Millie could have their own room and Chas moved back downstairs to the parlour. This worked very well for Chas who struggled with the stairs. A few weeks later Annie told her father that she was with child again, his fifth grandchild was due in August and he hoped Connie may also have some news. Frank was fit for work and had been taken on as a regular labourer for the railway company. He spent his days working up and down the lines or in the local stations, Ewell, Chessington, Tolworth, Surbiton, Thames Ditton and Hinchley Wood. He was excited about becoming a father again and looked forward to those early years that he had missed with his elder son. On the 8th August Charlie got the best birthday present he could ever have, a little baby brother called Percy Ronald, born the day before his own birthday. Chas was delighted to have a second grandson, despite the house being rather crowded and they had another little party to celebrate.

Sid was back working at the farm as a cowman and Millie in the laundry, Frank was on the railways and Annie gave up her cleaning job to look after Percy. Charlie Sherwood attended Tolworth Boys School in Red Lion Lane and Chas was content apart from a few aches and pains. Connie visited once a fortnight off the train from Wimbledon and usually brought kippers from the fish shop where she worked. Chas always sat at the front window while working on his baskets and when Connie appeared around the corner he would shout to Annie:

> *"Here comes kippers, put the kettle on."*

On Connie days they had a grand breakfast of bloaters with bread and butter, a pot of tea and a nice chat. Connie had always been the serious one, but she seemed even more distant than before. Annie was concerned and feared that Frank may have been right about her husband. Chas hoped that Connie may give him another grandchild but it was not to be, she gradually visited less and less because her husband wanted her to stay at home in Wimbledon.

Frank was always making things and asked Chas if he could build a pigeon loft next to the rabbit hutches. He thought it would be nice for the boys. Chas was happy for Frank to carry on, the rabbits had been a great success and he trusted Frank's judgement. Frank often went around to visit his mother Martha who lived in Thornhill Road and she knew all about racing pigeons, her father and brothers had all kept birds. Martha enjoyed Frank's visits and sometimes she would walk to Lenelby Road for Sunday tea. Martha was four years older than Chas and very sprightly, she was living on her pension of five shillings a week and did not always have enough money to buy food. She was usually sent home from the Plants with an armful of vegetables and a few sweet things to eat.

Frank drew out his plan and set about measuring up for the wood. Chas didn't use his shed for storing willow any more so Frank dismantled it and with the addition of some extra planks and a few pine lathes from Budd and Bird in King Charles Road he started the elaborate structure. Chas twisted some old willow that was no good for his baskets into stiff rods for the cage and after a couple of weeks the loft was ready for its tenants. Sid knew an elderly farmhand who raced pigeons and took Frank round to see him. He had a clutch of one dozen eggs due to hatch and Frank could have them along with a broody hen bird for the price of a laundry basket. Frank agreed and Chas was pleased to oblige. Charlie was interested right from the start and could not wait for the birds to hatch. The little fluffy chicks were brought into the kitchen to be kept warm by the oven which did not go down too well with Annie, but the boys loved them. Charlie helped Frank clean them out and Percy liked holding and stroking them even when he was a tiny tot.

The Pigeon Club met at The Red Lion once a month and Frank joined up. It was not long before he had birds old enough to race. Charlie loved being involved in the training, they ringed their legs and took them in baskets over to Newmans Farm to release them and checked how long it took the birds to find their way home. They gradually took them further and further away. Some got lost never to return but most did and a handful of birds were much quicker than others. The whole family took great delight in waiting on a Sunday afternoon to watch the birds flying back to roost. Charlie as he got older became very adept at identifying a good racer and started breeding

Frank & the Pigeon Loft about 1928.

from the best birds and with Frank's help also sold some stud cock birds. Chas liked the pigeons and was very proud of his grandson.

Percy spent a lot of time with his grandfather when his father was at work and his brother at school. Grandad Chas was always there to tell stories about millers and mariners and great derring-do. Percy was more practical than his brother and Chas taught him how to make small baskets, Percy was good at making things. Annie was always busy with housework, laundry or cooking. Sid and Millie were still living in the back bedroom and when Percy was three, Millie had a baby boy called Desmond Gordon. Sid was an extremely proud father and now Chas had six grandchildren, three girls and three boys. The house was getting rather crowded with Annie, Frank Charlie and Percy all sharing one bedroom and Sid, Millie and Des in the other. Chas could not climb the stairs now and lived the whole time in the front parlour or sat in the yard during fine weather.

Soon after Des was born, Sid was offered a job as head cowman at Longdown Farm in Ewell and the job came with a cottage. Sid had handed in his notice at Newmans Farm with a few days left to work. He was in the yard one morning when one of the young lads had gone in to feed the bull and it turned on him. Sid jumped into the pen with a pitchfork and kept stabbing the bull and dragged the lad out. He saved the boy's life and it made front page news in The Surrey Comet. Sid was a hero and Chas was so proud of his youngest son who was a very reluctant celebrity. Chas was sad to see Sid and his little family go but it was only a couple of miles away, close enough to visit and Chas still had his Annie with Charlie and Percy, not forgetting Frank of course who had become like a son to him.

Percy was now four years old and loved doing a bit of woodwork with his father. Frank took him down to Budd and Bird one Saturday morning to collect some timber for another shed. There was a small wiry dog lying on a large pile of straw by the office with three puppies snuggled up close to her. Percy sat and stroked the mother and talked gently to the puppies. Mrs Budd came out of the office and was amazed that Lily was not growling at Percy, she was very possessive of her pups. Percy asked if they could take a puppy home, Mrs Budd was more than happy to oblige and off they went with a little dog that squeaked all the way to Lenelby Road. Chas was delighted with the little creature and Percy was given the job of naming him. Pants, was Percy's best friend and when Percy was not around he would sit by Chas's feet in the front parlour. He grew into a sweet natured little terrier, a great ratter that loved digging and chasing rabbits and was not averse to catching the odd unwary pigeon.

Now that Sid had left there was more space in the house, Charlie and Percy went into the back room with Annie and Frank at the front. Pants slept downstairs with Chas in the front parlour. There was not much money coming in, Frank was the only breadwinner and Chas was getting five shillings a week pension. Annie needed to go out to work again and she found another cleaning job in Ravenswood Avenue not far from Mr Myers house.

Chas, like many other working men had hoped that Ramsay MacDonald, the country's first labour Prime Minister would make life better after the war, but things got worse. The miners were very militant and in May 1926 the whole country went out on General Strike for six months. Frank as a Transport and General Workers Union man could not work, they were living on Chas's pension and Annie's small earnings. There were food and fuel shortages, violent strike disputes and long dole queues including thousands of men, who had fought in The Great War and were unable to get work. It was the beginning of the great depression and times proved to be very hard for several years to come. This had a huge impact on Chas, his family were struggling to survive and his fear of the workhouse loomed large. He was determined to manage and keep his family together, however hard the struggle.

The following year Charlie was old enough to leave school and started work as a milk boy, it was very different from when his Uncle Percy trained thirty years earlier. The dairyman now walked alongside an enclosed horse drawn cart with crates of bottled milk, cream, cheese, butter and eggs. Charlie ran the milk to the doorsteps and picked up the empties. The dairyman observed that Charlie was very good at counting and could check change quickly. He was given more responsibility and after only three years he was given his own round and he made the most of it. He was really sharp and liked by his customers. His interest in racing pigeons had developed his knowledge of betting, he followed the horses, particularly at Epsom and started taking bets off his customers. He placed the bets in his own name and reimbursed his customers, minus his commission. This proved to be very lucrative and he gave his mother extra when he had a good week to buy the family a nice cut of meat off the black market or some special treats.

Chas worried about Charlie's interest in gambling and gave him the advice that Mr William had given him when he was twenty-one:

"Only bet once, on one race, once a year, to make it special."

Charlie listened and knew gambling was a fool's pastime but he could see the profit in managing the bets. He took bets off his family just once a year for The Derby and included himself. If they did well, they all celebrated with a party, if they did not, Charlie waived his commission. He always remembered grandad's advice and was very cautious when making a personal bet and only ever on the big races, The Derby, The Oaks, The Grand National and The Boat Race. Thirty years after Chas died, gambling rules were relaxed and Charles Frank Sherwood opened a betting office in Epsom where he made his fortune as a turf accountant.

Little Percy was seven years younger than his brother and born at the beginning of the depression when times were very hard and food was scarce, he was a little undernourished but otherwise a healthy lad. The same year that Charlie started work, Percy started school and he liked it very much. It was a long walk to Tolworth Boys but Percy didn't mind, he had a small gang of friends and they would all run along together. He was a bit scared of Mr Stokoe, the headmaster but he tried hard and was well liked by the teachers. His school report when he left at the age of 14 said:

> *"A very steady persevering boy, interested in his school and his work. Always trustworthy."*

Percy was one of the youngest in the class but got 10 out of 10 for all his written exams. His best subjects were Art, English Composition, Maths, Geography and History. He didn't like science and he hated sport. When Percy left school in 1934 he started work as a green grocer's errand boy but he was always more interested in the mechanics of the motorised delivery van that had replaced the horse and cart. He saved up to buy his own motorbike when he was sixteen and spent all his spare time tinkering in the back yard at Lenelby Road. His interest led to an apprenticeship at Fox and Nicholls, a garage on the Portsmouth Road that specialised in Lagondas and Bentleys. Percy eventually became a successful businessman like his brother but that is another story.

It was 1930 and Chas worried about what the future may hold for his grandchildren. The country was still in the grip of deep depression, unemployment had doubled and Oswald Mosley was causing unrest with his fascist propaganda. One hot sunny day, when he was sitting in the yard watching Charlie feeding the pigeons and Percy playing with Pants he thought, if he died tomorrow, his greatest achievement was his family, his eyes filled with tears. He was proud of his son Percy and his family even though he had never met his granddaughters. His eldest child Annie had always been there for him and was a good daughter, wife and mother. She was also great fun with her kind husband Frank and their two clever sons. Sid was happy with Millie and little Des just down the road in Ewell and Connie was independent with her own life. In August 1930 Chas became ill and took to his bed for most of the following days. Charlie was particularly concerned and sat with his grandad whenever he could. Pants also spent more time at his side and one morning, Annie rose to make breakfast and found Chas had died in his sleep on Friday the 4th September.

Charles Christopher Plant was seventy-five years old and died at home knowing that he had a loving family around him. Annie registered his death and arranged the funeral, he was buried at Surbiton Cemetery on the 9th September 1930 in plot 2898. He was joined by his son-in-law Frank, in 1956 and his beautiful daughter Annie, in 1958. He was a good husband and caring father who liked people and always had a sparkle in his eye. He left behind a happy family and that was all he ever wished for.

Annie with Percy about 1930.

Acknowledgements.

I would like to thank my husband Ken for patiently reading countless drafts and my oldest and constant friend Barbara for her thorough proof reading. They have both supported me throughout and encouraged me to keep going.